THE PERSONAL HERESY

Books by C. S. Lewis

A Grief Observed
George MacDonald: An Anthology
Mere Christianity
Miracles
The Abolition of Man
The Great Divorce
The Problem of Pain
The Screwtape Letters (with "Screwtape Proposes a Toast")
The Weight of Glory
The Four Loves
Till We Have Faces
Surprised by Joy: The Shape of My Early Life
Reflections on the Psalms
Letters to Malcolm, Chiefly on Prayer
The World's Last Night: And Other Essays
Poems
The Dark Tower: And Other Stories
Of Other Worlds: Essays and Stories
Narrative Poems
A Mind Awake: An Anthology of C. S. Lewis
Letters of C. S. Lewis
All My Road Before Me
The Business of Heaven: Daily Readings from C. S. Lewis
Present Concerns: Journalistic Essays
Spirits in Bondage: A Cycle of Lyrics
On Stories: And Other Essays on Literature

ALSO AVAILABLE FROM HarperCollins

The Chronicles of Narnia
The Magician's Nephew
The Lion, the Witch and the Wardrobe
The Horse and His Boy
Prince Caspian
The Voyage of the Dawn Treader
The Silver Chair
The Last Battle

THE PERSONAL HERESY

A CONTROVERSY

C. S. Lewis

AND E. M. W. TILLYARD

HarperOne
An Imprint of HarperCollinsPublishers

THE PERSONAL HERESY. Copyright © 1939 by C. S. Lewis Pte. Ltd. All rights reserved. Printed in the United States of America. No part of this book may be used or reproduced in any manner whatsoever without written permission except in the case of brief quotations embodied in critical articles and reviews. For information, address HarperCollins Publishers, 195 Broadway, New York, NY 10007.

HarperCollins books may be purchased for educational, business, or sales promotional use. For information, please email the Special Markets Department at SPsales@harpercollins.com.

Originally published in the United Kingdom in 1939 by Oxford University Press.

FIRST EDITION

Library of Congress Cataloging-in-Publication Data

Names: Lewis, C. S. (Clive Staples), 1898-1963, author. | Tillyard, E. M. W. (Eustace Mandeville Wetenhall), 1889-1962, author.
Title: The personal heresy : a controversy / C. S. Lewis and E. M. W. Tillyard.
Description: First edition. | New York, NY : HarperOne, 2017. | "Originally published as The Personal Heresy in the United Kingdom in 1939 by Oxford University Press" | 1939 edition had author E. M. W. Tillyard's name presented first on the title page.
Identifiers: LCCN 2016030647 | ISBN 9780062565624 (paperback) | ISBN 9780062565587 (e-book)
Subjects: LCSH: Poetry. | Criticism. | Authors and readers. | BISAC: RELIGION / Spirituality. | RELIGION / Christianity / Literature & the Arts. | RELIGION / Christianity / General.
Classification: LCC PN1031 .T455 2017 | DDC 808.1—dc23 LC record available at https://lccn.loc.gov/2016030647

CONTENTS

	PREFACE	VII
I	C. S. LEWIS	1
II	E. M. W. TILLYARD	37
III	C. S. LEWIS	59
IV	E. M. W. TILLYARD	85
V	C. S. LEWIS	117
VI	E. M. W. TILLYARD	149
	NOTE	177

PREFACE

The authors would like it to be understood that the following essays do not form what is usually called a 'symposium', that is, a staged or prearranged *débat, estrif,* or *disputatio* in which the combatants undertake respectively to maintain and attack a prescribed thesis for the delectation of the audience. The author of the first essay was not, when he wrote it, personally acquainted with his antagonist; he hoped, rather than expected, to be answered sometime and somewhere by 'any whom it might concern'. Since then the argument has continued by its momentum. The authors have decided to publish it because, thinking the subject worthy of consideration, they have not thought that they could lay it more fairly before their readers in any other way. No doubt this form has its drawbacks. Both authors have found now and then that the alley they were exploring was blind and have had to retrace their way, with apparent waste of time and effort. Further, they may be taxing the reader's attention more severely than if each had written a full-length book. But they believe that the ease with which either of these books might have been read—

specially by those who had never read, or had forgotten, the other—would be deceptive. The critical world is at present much divided into groups and camps, and those who accept their principles from any one camp are not, perhaps, always aware of what can be urged against them. One remembers the *Dumb Orators* in Crabbe. The readers of this book cannot fall into that error; bane and antidote here grow side by side; and neither author, even if he wished, can here play Cato to any 'little senate' of his own.

It has also seemed to us that a revival of the art of Controversy would now be a wholesome thing. A dangerous habit is growing up among critics of disagreeing without ever meeting face to face; of *taking for granted* in footnotes and parentheses and anonymous reviews the absurdity of opinions which have never, in fact, been publicly refuted. To all this we feel that the *justa controversio* stands much as the *duello* stands to mere backbiting, nose-slitting, and abuse; and is, for that reason, to be preferred.

It only remains to thank the English Association for allowing the reprint of the first three essays, which originally appeared in volumes xix (1934), xx (1935), and xxi (1936) of *Essays and Studies*.

E.M.W.T.
C.S.L.

I

> An inquisitiveness into the minutest circumstances and casual sayings of eminent contemporaries is indeed quite natural; but so are all our follies.
>
> COLERIDGE

During the war I saw an anthology which contained the work of some 'young soldier poets', as we used to call them. The advertisement on the wrapper promised that if you bought the book these young men would tell you things about themselves which they had never told to 'their fathers, or their sweethearts, or their friends'. The assumption was that to read poetry means to become acquainted with the poet, as we become acquainted with a man in intimate conversation, to steep ourselves in his personality; and the appeal based on this assumption was an appeal to curiosity. When that appeal is put so crudely, it endangers no educated reader's judgement; and if that assumption were made only in advertisements, it would not be worth consideration. But it is impossible not to recognize in the passage which I have quoted the logical conclusion of a tendency from which, in our own day, even reputable criticism is not always exempt. Few will deny that the role of biography in our literary studies is steadily increasing; and if we look into the most popular literary biographies of the last decade or so, we shall find that in them the poet's life is connected with his work after a fashion quite alien from the methods of Johnson. Poetry is widely believed to be the 'expression of personality': the end which we are supposed to pursue in reading it is a certain contact with the poet's soul; and 'Life' and 'Works' are simply two diverse expressions of this single quiddity. In a work published by His Majesty's Stationery Office we are urged to use English literature as 'a means of contact with great minds'.[1] This seems innocent enough, but there is more behind. In Dr Tillyard's *Milton* we are told that the only critics of *Paradise Lost* who 'seemed to tackle' the 'problem'—for a poem is always a 'problem' to psychological critics—in the 'right kind of way' were the Satanists; and their rectitude consisted, apparently, in the fact that they 'invested the character of Satan with all that Milton felt and valued most strongly'.[2] They were right because they assumed from the outset

---

[1] *The Teaching of English in England*, 1921, p. 15.
[2] *Milton*, E. M. W. Tillyard, 1930, p. 1.

that Milton's poetry must be the expression of his personality. Later in the book Dr Tillyard complains that such matters as style 'have concerned the critics far more than what the poem is really about, the true state of Milton's mind when he wrote it'.[3] The concealed major premise is plainly the proposition that all poetry is *about* the poet's state of mind. Certainly, in the opinion of Mr Kingsmill this proposition is so axiomatic that a poem which is *not* about the poet's state of mind can for that reason be condemned. Of *Sohrab and Rustum* he says, 'Throughout the interminable poem there is hardly a hint of any relation between Thomas and Matthew Arnold on the one hand, and Rustum and Sohrab on the other. Even in the death of Sohrab the emotional pressure behind the verse seems to me . . . *too weak* to suggest any conscious or unconscious recognition on Arnold's part of the likeness between his fate and Sohrab's.'[4] If the emotion were strong, apparently, it would have to be egoistic; if the poem were good, it would express the emotions arising out of the poet's personal situation. More difficult to interpret is Mr T. S. Eliot's statement that 'The rage of Dante . . . the deep surge of Shakespeare's general cyni-

---

[3] *Milton*, E. M. W. Tillyard, 1930, p. 237.
[4] *Matthew Arnold*, Hugh Kingsmill, 1928, p. 127. Italics mine.

cism and disillusionment, are *merely* gigantic attempts to metamorphose private failures and disappointments'.[5] Of this it would, perhaps, carry us too far to say that what we most desire to know of an 'attempt' is whether it failed or succeeded, and that 'metamorphosis' is a dark conception till we have asked 'Metamorphosis *into what*?' It concerns our present purpose more to notice the assumed, and concealed, major premise that the cynicism and disillusionment put into the mouths of some Shakespearian characters are Shakespeare's. Even dramatic poetry is tacitly assumed to be the expression of the poet's personality. Nor is it only among the νεωτερίζοντες that such a dogma hides. A critic of a different school, Professor Garrod, has admitted into his *Wordsworth* sentences which bear, if they do not invite, a dangerous interpretation. We are there told that 'a man's poetry is but a part of him';[6] and this, in some sense, is true. A poet does many other things in addition to composing poems. But Professor Garrod goes on to say that if, in reading poetry, 'we put the poet out of the room, we let in one of two interlopers. We let in either ourselves or a false image of the poet.' Professor Garrod's words, judged in the light of all he says else-

---

[5] *Selected Essays*, T. S. Eliot, 1923, p. 137. Italics mine.
[6] *Wordsworth*, H. W. Garrod, 2nd edition, 1927, p. 9.

where, may, perhaps, be so understood as not to involve the personal heresy. But it cannot be denied that they are most easily read as though they involved the assumption that what we attend to, in reading poetry, is a representation claiming to be the poet; and that to read poetry well is to have a true idea of the poet, while to read it ill is to have a false idea of him. Taken in this sense their implication seems to me to be a serious error.

In this paper I shall maintain that when we read poetry as poetry should be read, we have before us no representation which claims to be the poet, and frequently no representation of a *man*, a *character*, or a *personality* at all.

I shall begin by tackling the problem on a very shallow and popular level. Dismissing all the more ambiguous senses in which the word *personality* can be used, and in which we can be said to *meet* or *come into touch* with it, I shall try to show that there is at least one very obvious sense in which it is certain that the object offered to us by a good poem is not the poet's personality. My position—in this obvious sense, which will suffice at the present stage—is so simple that a few examples will make it good. I read, for instance,

> *Whenas in silks my Julia goes,*
> *Then, then, methinks how sweetly flows*
> *That liquefaction of her clothes.*

If the theory which I am attacking, taken in its crudest sense, were true, it ought to be true that what I derive from these lines is the impression of a certain personality. My pleasure ought to consist in the perception of that personality, and the permanent result of the poem ought to be an enrichment of my conception of human nature. Now there is no doubt that I can extract from the poem the idea of a humorous nature, amorous yet dainty, dowered with an almost feminine sensibility to the qualities of clothes. The question is whether that is presented to me as part of my poetical experience. For, of course, any and every result which may follow from my reading of a poem cannot be included in my poetical apprehension of it, and cannot, therefore, belong to the poem as a poem. Thus, for example, I can learn from reading these lines that the pronunciation 'clo'es' for *clothes* is at least as old as the date at which the poem was written. That piece of philological knowledge is a result of the poem; but clearly philological truths do not make part of the poem, nor do I encounter them so long as I am apprehending it with my imagination, but only when I come to reflect upon it, later, and in a very different light. The problem, therefore, is whether my perception of the poet's character is part of my direct experience of the poem, or whether it is simply one of those later and unpoetical results. I think this is answered as soon as it is asked. I know that the poet was sensitive to the qualities of silk. How? Plainly because he has conveyed them so vividly. But then he must have conveyed or expressed them to me *before* I can know that he was thus sensitive, and to say that he has conveyed them to me means that I myself, in reading the poem, became conscious of silk in a new way. I know that his expression is good only because that expression has already wrought its effect on me. I see that *liquefaction* is an admirably chosen word; but only because I have already found myself seeing silk as I never saw it before. The first object presented to me is an idea of silk. To account for the unusual vividness of that idea, I may then analyze the poem and conclude 'It is the word *liquefaction* that does the trick'; and only then, by a third step, can I conclude 'With what eyes he must have seen[7] silk to think of such a word', and thence 'He must have been that sort of man'. In other words, my idea of the poet presupposes that the poem has already had its effect on my imagination, and cannot, therefore, be part of that effect. The only experience which has any claim

---

[7] Throughout this discussion I use words such as *seeing* or *perception* to mean the *genus* of which sensation, knowing, opining, imagining, and the like are *species*. *Apprehension* would in some ways have been preferable, but it has intellectual implications. My own usage has, at any rate, the sanction of our ordinary habits of speech. *Having* would be the best of all, but would have required explanation.

to be poetical experience is an apprehension, not of the poet, but of silk. Perception of the poet's skill comes later, and could not come at all unless I had first and foremost apprehended the silk; and perception of the personality implied by such skill comes later yet. It is twice removed from the essential poetic experience.

But perhaps I seem to have chosen, unfairly, an example in which the poetry is of an unusually sensuous and simple type. In fact, however, the more subtle types of poetry differ only by being less manageable for purposes of exposition.

> *Very old are we men;*
>   *Our dreams are tales*
> *Told in dim Eden*
>   *By Eve's nightingales.*

Here it is very much harder to indicate by prose pointers the nature of the object presented to me. But at least we may be quite certain what it is not. It is not a picture of the poet. It is something extended interminably in time, shrouded in mystery, and yet, for all its age, carrying still about it some hint of the dewy freshness of primeval myth. That may not be a good description of the thing, but it would be a much worse description of Mr De la

Mare. If I try to imagine Mr De la Mare, I can imagine him only as an individual living in a particular time and place, with other times and places forming a sort of context that stretches away indefinitely on all sides of him. But what I look towards in reading the poem is that context itself—the ages of human history. How could the object be the idea of a man who himself is inside that context? Where the thing presented already contains the poet as one of its least important details, how could it also *be* the poet himself?

To be sure there are poems in which the thing that we attend to is unmistakably a human being in a certain state of emotion. Thus, for example,

> *I breathe again.*
> *Trances of thought and mountings of the mind*
> *Come fast upon me. It is shaken off,*
> *That burthen of my own unnatural self,*
> *The heavy weight of many a weary day*
> *Not mine, and such as were not made for me.*

Such lines might seem to support the case of my opponents; for beyond question what they convey to me is the keener awareness of a certain kind of human feeling—just as Herrick's poem enabled me to see the liquid quality of silk as I had never seen it before. But the difficulty is only apparent. It is easy to suppose that we do not know whether these lines come from a work where the poet is speaking in his own person or from a speech by one of the characters in a play. And it is clear that if they came from a play they would not directly present us with the poet's character. The Drama is, in fact, the strongest witness for my contention. Even my convinced opponents would falter in dealing with the Drama, for there the poet is manifestly out of sight, and we attend not to him but to his creations. How far any of them may resemble him is, no doubt, an interesting question; but to ask that question, still more to answer it, is clearly to have turned from imaginative apprehension to later and unpoetic reflection. The objective or impersonal theory of poetry which I am defending finds its easiest application in the drama and the epic. And if we return, with this in our minds, to the passage under consideration, we must surely agree that there is nothing in the poetry itself to show whether it is dramatic or not. We happen to know that it is from Wordsworth's *Prelude*. But we do not know that by imaginative experience. Or if we take the *Prelude* as a whole, the appreciation of it as poetry does not include the knowledge that it is autobiographical. A process of human development, that is, a particular man growing up, is presented to us; that this man is, or is intended to be, Wordsworth himself, we learn from literary history—unless we are so simple as to suppose that the use of the first person settles the question. The same holds good of all poetry. We do not know whether the story of the sonnets was Shakespeare's own story or not; we do not know whether Milton really grieved for the death of Mr King or not; and if we know that Shelley had really met Keats, we do not know it in and by appreciating *Adonais*. So that at the very best, all we can mean by claiming to find the poet's personality in a poem is that we find some personality, which may, on quite other grounds, be discovered to be that of the poet. I submit that this is not what is ordinarily meant by *knowing* or *getting into touch with* a man. If I have the idea of a particular character, and it just happens that a man, say, in Timbuctoo exists who does, as a matter of fact, bear that character—a man I have never heard of—it would be a very odd use of language to say that I knew, or was in touch with, the man as soon as I had the idea. At best, therefore, we meet the poet, even in the most personal lyric poetry, only in a strained and ambiguous sense. But we can go much farther than this. It is, in fact, quite impossible that the character represented in the poem should be identically the same with that of the poet. The character presented is that of a man in the grip of this or that emotion: the real poet is a man who has already escaped from that emotion sufficiently to see it objectively—I had almost said to see it dramatically—and to make poetry of it. The man who cries out with pain is not the same as the man who vividly expresses to us the blood-curdling nature of the cry. The man who expends his spirit in a waste of shame is not the same as the man who sees the imaginative significance of that whole situation and writes down 'The expense of spirit in a waste of shame'. The characteristic of a poet is, after all that he is a poet; and if poems put us into touch with him, the characters presented to us in all poems, however diverse they may be, ought, at least, to have this in common, that they are all poets. But the great crowd of lovers, mourners, fighters, and the like whom we meet in sonnets and songs are not poets. They may be spoken of in the first person, but they differ from their creators by this very fact that they are merely loving, mourning, and being angry; whereas the real poet is writing poetry about love, or sorrow, or anger. Nor, indeed, is it possible for any one to describe himself, even in prose, without making of himself, to some extent, a dramatic creation. The character whom I describe as myself leaves out; at least, this present act of description—which is an element in my real history; and that is the beginning of a rift which will grow wider at every step we take from the vulgarity of confession to the disinfected and severer world of lyric poetry. The 'I' and 'me' of whom poets speak really affect us in exactly the same way as any of the other characters whom they present to us; they are phases of human nature, detached from their historical context—οἷα ἂν γένοιτο—things that might happen. That something tolerably like them has actually happened in the poet himself is poetically irrelevant.

It follows, then, at least in the crudest and most obvious sense of the words, that the thing presented to us in any poem is not and never can be the personality of the poet. It is the liquid movement of silk, or the age and mystery of man, or a particular man escaping from a long period of constraint—never Wordsworth, or De la Mare, or Herrick. But here a distinction must be made. Poetry, after all, is not science or history; and the silks are not described in the manner of the mercer, nor the history of man after the manner of the anthropologist. It is, in fact, these things, not as they are, but as they seem to be, which poetry represents to me; or so I shall be told. It may be true that what I am aware of in reading Herrick's poem is silk, but it is not silk as an object *in rerum natura*. I see it as Herrick saw it; and in so doing, it may be argued, I do come into contact with his temperament in the most intimate—perhaps in the only possible—way. For the moment I not only accept but embrace this view of the matter. It introduces a point of the last importance which the crudest form of the personal theory had overlooked. Let it be granted that I do approach the poet; at least I do it by sharing his consciousness, not by studying it. I look with his eyes, not at him. He, for the moment, will be precisely what I do not see; for you can see any eyes rather than the pair you see with, and if you want to examine your own glasses you must take them off your own nose. The poet is not a man who asks me to look at *him;* he is a man who says 'look at that' and points; the more I follow the pointing of his finger the less I can possibly see of *him*. To be sure there are all sorts of difficult questions hanging over us. But for the moment let us thrust them aside. Whatever may turn out to be the whole truth, let us make fast, before we go a step farther, this aspect of the truth. To see things as the poet sees them I must share his consciousness and not attend to it; I must look where he looks and not turn round to face him; I must make of him not a spectacle but a pair of spectacles: in fine, as Professor Alexander would say, I must *enjoy* him and not *contemplate* him. Such is the first positive result of my inquiry.

Having grasped this truth, I proceed to a second question. What is the nature of this consciousness which I come to share but not to study, to look *through* but not look *at,* in appreciating a poem? The personal theory will hold that the consciousness in question is that of the poet, considered as an individual, contingent, human specimen. Mr Smith sees things in one way; Mr Jones sees them in another; Mr Wordsworth sees them in a third. What we share in reading Wordsworth is just Wordsworth's point of view as it happens to exist in him as a psychological fact; and that is why modern criticism attends so willingly to psychology and biography. And as long as we are dealing with romantic poets not far removed from us in time, this view of the matter is not unplausible. It cannot, however, have escaped any one's attention that there is a whole class of poetical experiences in which the consciousness that we share cannot possibly be attributed to any single human individual. Let us consider an example.

> And Babylon, the glory of kingdoms, the beauty of the Chaldees' excellency, shall be as when God overthrew Sodom and Gomorrah. It shall never be inhabited, neither shall it be dwelt in from generation to generation: neither shall the Arabian pitch tent there; neither shall the shepherds make their fold there. But wild beasts of the desert shall lie there; and their houses shall be full of doleful creatures; and owls shall dwell

there, and satyrs shall dance there. And the wild beasts of the islands shall cry in their desolate houses, and dragons in their pleasant palaces.

It does not greatly matter how highly the reader values the imaginative impression produced upon him by these words: that they produce some imaginative impression, that he comes to enjoy a new and heightened mode of consciousness in reading them, will not be denied. The question arises whose consciousness it is. Who was the man to whom this mode belonged, the man whose personality or temperament we are coming to share?

Very little argument suffices to show that it cannot have been the original author. The mood to which we are introduced by these lines was not only not normal in the Hebrew writer; it did not and could not exist in him at all. To begin with 'doleful creatures', 'owls', 'satyrs', 'wild beasts of the islands', and 'dragons' are mere mistranslations. Whatever they evoke or express was wholly absent from the mind of the author, and, what is worse, other things were there in its place. Only the crudest view of the relations between language and imagination could lead us to suppose that the experience which lacked these words and used others in their place was at all like the experience of the modern reader. But that is not all. The theme of the whole passage is

Babylon and the fall of Babylon. Now the *sound* Babylon did not exist in the original: yet that sound counts for a great deal in our experience of the passage. Babylon: the very word is like a bell. But Isaiah—or whoever it was—never heard that bell toll. He may have heard a better bell, but that is nothing to the purpose. If we turn from the sound to the idea—we may grant that false abstraction for the argument's sake—the rift between our mood and that of the original becomes even wider. For us Babylon is far away and long ago; it comes to us through the medium of centuries of poetry about the East and about antiquity; it comes to us as descendants of those Germanic poets who had from the first a romantic and elegiac delight in the ruin and decay of greatness. We have read of Troy, too, and perhaps, in our salad days, we loved the courts where Jamshid gloried and drank deep. Now Babylon, to the writer, was neither long ago nor far away. Its greatness was not the cloudy greatness of old empires fallen in the past, but the oppressive greatness of an enemy and a neighbour. He felt about Babylon not as we feel about Troy and Nineveh, but as some Indian nationalists may feel about London. The poetry of Babylon, for us, belongs to the same world as

> *But all about the rugged walls were hung*
> *With riven moniments of time forepast.*

The poetry, for him, belonged rather to the world of

When we've wound up the watch on the Rhine.

And with this, presumably, analysis may rest. It is obvious that no two experiences could be more grotesquely unlike than that of the writer, and that of the modern reader, of this passage. Nor shall we fare much better if we turn from the original writer to the translator. No one who has himself ever tried to translate will doubt that what was uppermost in the mind of the translator as he wrote was the problem of translation itself. When he wrote 'dragons' he was not inquiring whether this completed the picture or expressed his emotion, but whether it rendered the Hebrew. Nor did he look at the Hebrew itself aesthetically; he worked in fear and trembling to transmit without loss what he believed to be the literal record of the word of God. Even if some imaginative element crept in amidst his philological and theological preoccupations, it must have differed essentially from that which we enjoy; for as his English version grew he had the Hebrew always before him, and was thus inevitably involved in a work of comparison which has no parallel in our experience of the passage.

The result, then, is this. Such a passage gives us imaginative experience. In having that experience we do come to share or enjoy a new kind of consciousness, but that consciousness is not the consciousness of any single individual. And it will be plain that the passage I have chosen is only one of a very large class. Wherever we have traditional poetry there will be epithets and metrical devices which are the offspring of no single human temperament; wherever we have ancient poetry at all, there will be language which was commonplace to the writers but which time has turned into beauty; wherever we get misunderstanding—as in the common, beautiful, mistranslation of Virgil's *lacrimae rerum*—there will be poetry that no poet wrote. Every work of art that lasts long in the world is continually taking on these new colours which the artist neither foresaw nor intended. We may, as scholars, detect, and endeavour to exclude, them. We may, as critics, decide that such adventitious beauties are in a given case meretricious and trivial compared with those which the artist deliberately wrought. But all that is beside the purpose. Great or small, fortunate or unfortunate, they have been poetically enjoyed. And that is enough for my purpose. There can be poetry without a poet. We can have poetic experience which does not consist in sharing the 'personality' of a poet. To be encrusted with such poetless poetry is the reward, or the penalty, of every poem that endures. *Miratur non sua poma.*

It will be said that in such cases it is we who make the poetry. It is our own temperament that we enjoy. But surely not our normal or daily temperament? I do not perceive the fall of Babylon in that way whenever I think of it. The kind of seeing that we enjoy in reading ancient poetry arises only when the stimulus of the right word is applied. That it is mine while I enjoy it no one will deny. Even on the personal view, when I come to share, or to look through, the mind of the poet, his mind becomes mine, in so far as, and as long as, I succeed in appreciating his poem. What else do we mean by 'sharing'? We shall all agree that when my way of seeing things is altered by reading a poem, it is *my* way of seeing them that is altered. The real question is whether this alteration always (or ever) consists in my coming to share the personal point of view of the man whom we call the poet. And our examples show that this is at any rate not always the case. It does at least sometimes happen that the new 'personality' or 'point of view' whereby we respond to the poem never existed in the poet. Whether it is 'ours' or not is largely a question of words. It is certainly not 'ours' in the sense of being normal to us, or typical of us. No less certainly it is 'ours' while we read: that is what is meant when we say that the poem creates it in *us*. But this is beside the purpose.

What now remains of the personal dogma? We have seen

reason to reject the view that in reading poetry we were presented with some object that could be described as 'the poet's personality'. At best we 'shared' or 'looked through' his personality *at* something else. But even this would not serve as a description of poetry in general; for we saw that in many cases the personality—if you still want to call it so—which we came to share was not that of any single human being. It was not, in fact, the personality of a person. More explicitly, it was not a personality at all. It was a mood, or a mode of consciousness, created temporarily in the minds of various readers by the suggestive qualities which certain words and ideas have taken on in the course of human history,[8] and never, so far as we know, existing normally or permanently—never constituting the *person*—in any one. We will postpone for a moment all inquiry into the nature of this abnormal mode of consciousness. We have seen that in the case of poetless poetry it cannot be personal. It remains to show that it is equally impersonal even when we have a single, conscious poet to deal with.

---

[8] I limit myself to what most concerns our present purpose. A full account would have to deal with the evocative qualities of word-order and construction, and also with *sounds*. The former are habitually neglected; the latter as habitually exaggerated. Critics without a phonetic training, being quite unable even to *hear* accurately the sound of their mother-tongue, are naturally most prone (*omne ignotum pro magnifico*) to attribute to mere sound all sorts of powers which it does not possess.

Once again I will take a familiar example. We must choose old, uncontroverted poetry for our laboratory work, or we shall darken counsel. The more exciting application of our views to our own favourites, or to contemporary work, may come later. Let us take a piece of Keats.

> *As when, upon a tranced summer-night,*
> *Those green-rob'd senators of mighty woods,*
> *Tall oaks, branch-charmed by the earnest stars,*
> *Dream, and so dream all night without a stir,*
> *Save from one gradual solitary gust*
> *Which comes upon the silence, and dies off,*
> *As if the ebbing air had but one wave.*

After what has been said I need not repeat that the object presented to us while we read these lines is not the man Keats. It is a wood: but a wood seen with other eyes than those we enjoy every day. As to the means by which we gain these new eyes, I take it there is no great mystery in principle, though there may be some dispute as to the details. We have, in the first place, the names of familiar *sensibilia*—*summer, night, wood, oak, stars, gust, air*— each of which, simply as it stands, calls up its proper associations. But these groups of association—these clusters of incipient imagery—affect one another. To take what is most obvious, 'night' is changed by its proximity to 'summer', and vice versa. It is not 'summer' *plus* 'night' *plus* 'oaks', &c. Each is what it is in virtue of its place among all the rest; and the mere placing of these words would in itself amount to a rough-and-ready suggestion of the total object to be presented. The poet might conceivably stop at the string of names. But notice, even at this level, what he would be doing. He would be selecting elements of common experience and arranging them in a special order, an order in which each transformed and coloured each. It is absolutely essential that each word should suggest not what is private and personal to the poet but what is public, common, impersonal, objective.[9] The common world with its nights, its oaks, and its stars, which we have all seen, and which mean at least *something* the same to all

---

[9] I am speaking of *what is imagined,* not of the *image* or *mental picture.* That the two are distinct is proved by the fact that very adequate, or even fine, imagining may go with very inadequate images. We all enjoy *Hero and Leander,* and this implies that we all succeed in *imagining* beautiful human bodies; but only extreme visualists, and, among them, only persons of considerable artistic training, have *images* of the human body which would stand examination. Those who share with the present writer a lively visualizing power can testify that this unruly faculty is as often the enemy as the servant of imagination; just as elaborate and 'realistic' toys hinder rather than help children in their play. The poet may give all his readers a common *imaginatum:* he is not to aim at giving them identical *imagines.*

of us, is the bank on which he draws his cheques. But the arrangement—the experiencing them together in that particular order—this at least, you may argue, is his own. To be sure the arrangement is his own in some sense: we shall see in a moment what to make of that. Let us first finish our analysis. If we turn to the more obviously 'poetical' elements we find the same principle at work. 'Tranced' goes beyond the sensible. What is here placed in juxtaposition with the 'summer night' is not another fragment from the visible world, but a fragment from the world of religious history, or psychology. Such power as it has depends again on the publicity of that world; and 'tranced' fails, if it does fail, precisely because its world is not sufficiently common. Trance is not a phenomenon whose meaning is quite sufficiently established; it does not mean the same to us all. In the next line ('green-rob'd senators') the whole idea of republican Rome, another common possession of the educated world, is called up, in order that these senators may bring the sudden flavour of their silence and grandeur out of Plutarch and Livy, and that this, set for a moment beside the trees, may make them a little different. What the idea of senator happens to mean to Keats and Keats only, or to me and me only, in virtue of our several psychological accidents, is precisely what does not count. What is used for the poem is the significance which they have for every one; their objective characteristics as real elements in the drama of history—in other words their place not in any individual's memory but in the memory of Europe. It is not relevant that Keats first read about senators (let us say) in a little brown book, in a room smelling of boiled beef, the same day that he pulled out a loose tooth; it is relevant that the senators sat still when the invading Gauls entered the Senate House; it is relevant that Rome really established an empire. With 'branch-charmed by the earnest stars' the sources are more complex. 'Charmed' brings in the idea of magic. There, again, we are on common ground. We have dipped again into the storehouse of public history. But this is instantly modified by the word *branch*. Here we are thrown back on sense. We have seen the trees with branches stretched up in intense stillness towards the stars. We have imagined or been told of people compelled by magical charms to stand as still as the trees. Lay the two side by side and add the word *earnest*—which is exactly the point where the sensible image and the idea of insensible 'magic' merge beyond hope of distinction—and the whole, like meeting drops of quicksilver, becomes a single perception. We see the thing in a new way; because the poet has found the proper scraps of ordinary seeing which, when put together, will unite into a new and extraordinary seeing.

Now these scraps or atoms of common experience, before they were united, were, as we have seen, no more personal to the poet than to any other man who has grown up in modern Europe. No doubt they are not quite the same in one man as in another. But it is just in so far as they approach sameness that they are useful for poetry. It is the resemblances between my stars and trees and senators and those of Keats, not the difference, that matters. In the elements, therefore, we should seek in vain the 'personality' of the poet. Let us ask, then, whether this personality is to be found in their arrangement. In other words, is the poet a man who sees each sensible object thus set off and illuminated by those contexts which they have in the poem?

In one sense the answer is plainly 'Yes'. While he is writing the poem, Keats certainly does see the trees modified by the senators and the charms of the earnest stars. But then so do we, while we read. But to say that Keats is capable of attaining such perception for a few moments by the exercise of his art is hardly to say that it is personal to him, that it makes part of his nature or temperament. Certainly, what the exponents of the personal dogma have in mind is something very much more than this. There is a widely spread belief that the poet is a man who habitually sees things in a special way, and that his metaphor and other technique are simply *means* by which he admits us to share for a moment what is normal with him. Now this is really quite untenable. The dilemma is as follows: are senators normally present to Keats whenever he sees, or thinks of, oaks? If they are not, then his normal consciousness of oaks is other than that which we come to enjoy in reading his poem. It is quite impossible that a perception which did not include the senators should be the same with one that did. We deceive ourselves if we suppose that Keats's 'senators' or Herrick's 'liquefaction' are mere substitutes for something else, un-senatorial and un-liquid, which was present in the poet's original perception and which he conveys to us by these, as by mere devices. It is a principle in architecture that nothing is great or small save by position. It is a principle of decoration that every colour is what it is only in virtue of the surrounding colours. It is a principle of thought that every proposition depends for its value upon the context. No less certainly every perception is what it is by virtue of its context; and without that context the single perception is an abstraction. To see trees and to think of the price of timber means seeing trees in one way; to think of the forests in romance means to see trees in a second way; and to think of senators in a third. Keats could not have seen his trees as we see them in reading *Hyperion* before he thought of the senators. To ask, then, whether he normally saw them thus is simply to ask whether he normally associated them with the senatorial idea. To ask in general if poets express their personality in their poetry is to ask whether they habitually live clothed in all that panoply of metaphor and rhythm which they use for their work: whether the dancer, as Sir Toby suggested, goes to church in a sink-a-pace and comes home in a coranto. The poets themselves supply the answer. From Homer invoking the Muse down to Herrick prosaically noting that every day is not good for verses—from the romantic talking of his 'genius' to Emerson declaring that there was a great deal of inspiration in a chest of good tea—they all unequivocally declare that the words (and a perception expressed in other words is another perception) will not come for the asking, are rare and wooed with hard labour, are by no means the normal furniture of the poet's mind, are least of all his own possession, his daily temper and habitual self. And even if the poets did not tell us this in so many words, they have betrayed themselves by their rough copies. The very passage which I have just quoted from Keats did not always exist in its present perfection. Keats had to grope for his

> *gradual solitary gust*
> *Which comes upon the silence, and dies off,*
> *As if the ebbing air had but one wave.*

But to grope for the words was to grope for the perception, for the one lives only in the other. Keats lacked this perception when he began to write. It was therefore no permanent element in his psychology, nor even in his poetic psychology. He had to bring it into existence; and what created it in him was the very same cause that creates it in us—the words, incarnating common experiences and juxtaposed so as to make new experience. Both for Keats and for us the heightened consciousness is something foreign, something won from without, from the boundless ocean of racial, not personal, perception. There is indeed a momentous difference between him and us. He actually won it; we only enjoy and applaud the conquest. But this difference must not mislead us. There is a great difference between a skilled hunter who can catch the game and a hungry cripple who can only eat it. But you must not on that account mistake the hunter for the hart; still less for Pan.

A critic on whom I was pressing this doctrine once replied to me, 'But if one hunter always brought back hart, and another always boar, I should begin to suspect a difference'. The objection warns me of a possible misunderstanding. What game the hunter kills is indeed determined by his time and place of hunting, by his skill and by his choice, and thus by the whole scheme of things—within which scheme his personality finds an important, though not an all-important, place. If the Personal Dogma asserted only that the poets hunt diverse game, and that this diversity is determined *inter alia* by their personalities, I should have no quarrel with it. But when the hunter is held to create the game, when the qualities of the venison set before me are traced all to the hunter and none to Pan, when I am advised to eat, not because it is good food according to the universal rules of human nourishment, but because I may thus become better acquainted with the huntsman, it is then that I must tell my hosts roundly that they know neither how to feed a man nor how to reverence the gods. I do not ask that those who agree with me should deny the essential difference between the poetry of Shakespeare and the poetry of Racine. I do not even object to their talking of it, when convenience so dictates, as a difference of personality. I will even consent to speak of the Racinity of Racine, and the Shakespearianity of Shakespeare: only, let us remember what we mean. Let us remember that their poethood consists not in the fact that each approached the universal world from his own angle (all men do that), but in their power of telling us what things are severally to be seen from those angles. To use their poetry is to attend to what they show us, to look, as I have said before, not at them, but through them at the world. To say that they show us different things is not to say that they are creating what they show us, out of their personalities, but only that they are both finite. Even the reports of two scouts in war differ, and that with a difference traceable to personality: for the braver man goes farther and sees more; but the *value* of his report by no means consists in the fact that the intelligence officer, while he receives it, has the pleasure of meeting a brave man. Even two opposite windows in my room will give me two different landscapes; and you may say, in a sense, that the landscape 'expresses' the nature and position of the window. But windows are not put there that you may study windows; rather that you may forget windows. And if you find that you are forced to attend to the glass rather than the landscape, then either the window or your eye is faulty.

A poet does what no one else can do: what, perhaps, no other poet can do; but he does not express his personality. His own personality is his starting-point, and his limitation: it is analogous to the position of the window or the degree of courage in the scout. If he remains at his starting-point he is no poet: as long as he is (like the rest of us) a mere personality, all is still to do. It is his business, starting from his own mode of consciousness, whatever that may happen to be, to find that arrangement of public experiences, embodied in words, which will admit him (and incidentally us) to a new mode of consciousness. He proceeds partly by instinct, partly by following the tradition of his predecessors, but very largely by the method of trial and error; and the result, when it comes, is for him, no less than for us, an acquisition, a voyage beyond the limits of his personal point of view, an annihilation of the brute fact of his own particular psychology rather than its assertion.

The objects, then, which we contemplate in reading poetry are not the private furniture of the poet's mind. The mind through which we see them is not his. If you ask whose it is, I reply that we have no reason to suppose that it is any one's. It comes into existence, here and there, for moments, in varying degrees: that it exists anywhere permanently and as a whole—that it anywhere forms a *person*—is an unnecessary hypothesis. But if it did, that person would not be a human being. A mind which habitually saw as synthetically—which saw each single object with so vast a context—as we are made to see for moments by poetry, would be as far removed from us as we are from the brutes. It would not, indeed, be the Divine Mind, for it apprehends only the *what* and ignores the *that;* whereas God must be a permanent philosopher no less than a permanent poet. But it would be a mind, none the less, greatly beyond the human. The ancients called it the Muse. That she exists is a needless hypothesis, though, for all I know, not an absurd one. At all events, only in her will personal critics find the haven they seek. Much criticism is faced with this dilemma. It asserts of poetry superhuman attributes: it believes in no superhuman subjects to support them. But with these speculations as to what the poetic consciousness *would be* if it existed anywhere as a permanent whole, criticism is not at all concerned. The personal dogma can be refuted without any inquiry into the nature of that mode of consciousness which it mistook for the poet's personality. And it will add faith to the refutation if we can ascribe causes for the error. One cause is not far to seek. In an age when many have to talk of poetry, this personal view offers obvious advantages. Very few care for beauty; but any one can be interested in gossip. There is always the great vulgar anxious to know what the famous man ate and drank and what he said on his deathbed; there is always the small vulgar greedy to lick up a scandal, to find out that the famous man was no better than he should be. To such people any excuse for shutting up the terrible books with all the lines and lines of verse in them and getting down to the snug or piquant details of a human life, will always be welcome. But there is a deeper reason than this. The personal dogma springs from an inability which most moderns feel to make up their minds between two alternatives. A materialist, and a spiritual, theory of the universe are both equally fatal to it; but in the coming and going of the mind between the two it finds its opportunity. For the typical modern critic is usually a half-hearted materialist. He accepts, or thinks he accepts, that picture of the world which popularized science gives him. He thinks that everything except the buzzing electrons is subjective fancy; and he therefore believes that all poetry must come out of the poet's head and express (of course) his pure, uncontaminated, undivided 'personality', because outside the poet's head there is nothing but the interplay of blind forces. But he forgets that if materialism is true, there is nothing else inside the poet's head either. For a consistent materialism, the poetless poetry for which I contend, and the most seemingly self-expressive 'human document', are equally the accidental[10] results of impersonal and irrational causes. And if this is so, if the sensation (Professor Housman has told us about it) which we call 'enjoying poetry' in no case betokens that we are really in the presence of purpose and spirituality, then there is no foothold left for the personal heresy. All poetry will indeed *suggest* something more than the collision of blind forces; but

---

[10] In order to avoid misunderstanding, I had better say that by 'accidental' I do not mean contingent, but 'undesigned'.

the suggestion will, in every case alike, be false. And why should this false suggestion arise from the movements in the things we call brains rather than from any other movements? It is just as likely to arise from historical accidents of language, or from printers' errors. If, on the other hand, something like Theism or Platonism or Absolute Idealism is true—if the universe is not blind or mechanical, then equally the human individual can have no monopoly in producing poetry. For on this view all is designed, all is significant. The poetry produced by impersonal causes is not illusory. The Muse may speak through any instrument she chooses.

Surely the dilemma is plain. Either there is significance in the whole process of things as well as in human activity, or there is no significance in human activity itself. It is an idle dream, at once cowardly and arrogant, that we can withdraw the human soul, as a mere epiphenomenon, from a universe of idiotic force, and yet hope, after that, to find for her some *faubourg* where she can keep a mock court in exile. You cannot have it both ways. If the world is meaningless, then so are we; if we mean something, we do not mean alone. Embrace either alternative, and you are free of the personal heresy.

II

In his brilliant essay on *The Personal Heresy in Criticism* printed in last year's *Essays and Studies of the English Association*, Mr C. S. Lewis mentioned my *Milton* as a book in which poetry was treated as the expression of personality. And up to a point he may have been right. But as he is hostile to my supposed way of thinking, and as I agree with a good deal of his essay, it seems either that I did not make myself clear or that Mr Lewis is not entirely right. So I welcome this opportunity of saying what I mean by personality in literature. However, though certain cross-purposes may be straightened by further discussion, I do not say that much of Mr Lewis's essay is not extremely provocative and controversial. With some of it I disagree; and as the matters of disagreement seem to me well worth dwelling on, I offer the comments that follow. I hope that my being stirred to argue the point with Mr Lewis may be taken as my warm tribute to his essay's excellence.

As a preliminary, I must express surprise that Mr Lewis considers the personal heresy, as he calls it, a sign of modernity. I should have thought it slightly shop-soiled.

Mr Lewis quotes an ambiguous passage from Mr T. S. Eliot as supporting it: yet what weight can this passage have in the face of so uncompromising an attack on the personal heresy as that author's essay on *Tradition and the Individual Talent*? Here Mr Eliot says that 'the progress of an artist is a continual self-sacrifice, a continual extinction of personality', and that 'honest criticism and sensitive appreciation is directed not upon the poet but upon the poetry'. And he comes to the conclusion that for the poet the mind of Europe and of his own country is much more important than his own private mind. Now these sentiments are not only close to Mr Lewis's but they agree with a strong modern tendency, whose limits are not easily drawn, to belittle the individual in comparison with the race, the personal in comparison with the abstract, the Renaissance in comparison with Byzantium. Whatever the fate of this tendency—it may peter out in a few years for all we can tell—at the moment it is modern, and the opposite tendency to cling to the personal, even if fated shortly to prevail, just fails to be modern.

As a second preliminary let me say I entirely accept Mr Lewis's contention that in the matter of personality you can draw no line between lyric and dramatic poetry. I believe with him that there is a difference between (for example) the poet's feeling towards personal pain and towards pain pictured in his poetry; but within the latter category it makes no difference whether the pain is pictured as happening to the poet speaking for himself in a lyric or to a fictitious personage in a drama.

To turn now to the words *personal* and *personality*, it is plain how easy misunderstanding may be if we consider the following sentence of Mr Lewis's. In commenting on the passage from Keats's *Hyperion* beginning—

> *As when, upon a tranced summer-night,*
> *Those green-rob'd senators of mighty woods,*
> *Tall oaks...*

he writes:

> It is not relevant that Keats first read about senators (let us say) in a little brown book, in a room smelling of boiled beef, the same day that he pulled out a loose tooth; it is relevant that the senators sat still when the invading Gauls entered the Senate House; it is relevant that Rome really established an empire.

In this passage Mr Lewis implies that 'personal' as a critical term includes every accident however trivial connected with the author. No one can complain that he does so, but I should guess that not a few supporters of the 'personal heresy' would simply ignore such trivialities in their conception of personality. They would attach them to the sphere of literary gossip, not to that of criticism. Certainly I should never dream of giving them any critical value in themselves and I should agree that to recall such things when reading poetry would be grossly inappropriate. The most that literary gossip can do in the way of criticism is to keep people off a wrong track. There is a story about Milton that once after his blindness, hearing a lady sing, he said, 'Now I swear this lady is handsome'. Such an anecdote might have had a critical use at the time when Milton was imagined to be insusceptible to female charm. Now that this error has been generally discarded, the anecdote has no critical value—it is no more than a pleasant piece of literary gossip, and to be conscious of it when we read, for instance, the Chorus's description of Dalila entering like a ship with streamers flying is to abuse both the anecdote and the poetry. If Mr Lewis in attacking the personal heresy is wishing to point out that some of the labour spent in recent years on Johnson and Lamb, for instance, is anecdotal rather than critical, and that to confound the two spheres is a heresy, then he has my support.

Of course Mr Lewis does not confine 'personal' to this trivial or accidental sense. He grants that it is possible through poetry to come into contact with a poet's temperament in the most intimate way. The reader shares the poet's consciousness. But, according to Mr Lewis, even so the personal contact involved is relatively unimportant: first, because the personality with which the reader achieves contact is not the poet's normal personality but a heightened, temporary, perhaps alien, personality; secondly, because that personality is a means of vision rather than the thing ultimately seen. The personal heresy consists in the reader's seeing the poet's *normal* personality in his poetry, and in focusing his eyes on that personality instead of letting them contemplate the universe in a particular way.

Now if it is heretical to hold that part of the value of poetry consists in gaining contact with the normal personality of the poet, then I am a heretic. But I shall probably be using the word *normal* in a way Mr Lewis would disclaim. When he imagines Keats reading about senators in a little brown book in a room smelling of boiled beef he attaches these supposed facts to Keats's normal personality. I should do nothing of the sort, but call them as irrelevant to his normal personality as to the passage of *Hyperion* under discussion. In other words by 'personality' or 'normal personality' I do not mean practical or everyday personality, I mean rather some mental pattern which makes Keats Keats and not Mr Smith or Mr Jones. (*Pattern* is of course a bad word because it implies the static, whereas personality cannot remain fixed: the poet's personality is in the pattern of the sea rather than in that of a mosaic pavement.) And I believe we read Keats in some measure because his poetry gives a version of a remarkable personality of which another version is his life. The two versions are not the same but they are analogous. Part of our response to poetry is in fact similar to the stirring we experience when we meet some one whose personality impresses us. Such a person may startle us by the things he does, but quite outside anything he does there will be a distinction about him which, though difficult to define, we prize and which has the faculty of rousing us to some extent from our quotidian selves. This person may be subject to accidents, such as toothache, irregular habits, or an uncertain temper, which interfere with our enjoying this distinguished mental pattern of his; yet we know that the pattern is there. Though subject to change it is definite enough to be called habitual; it can indeed be looked on as his normal self underlying the accidents of quotidian existence.

One of the readiest ways of pointing to the function of personality in poetry is by means of the word *style*. *Style* readily suggests the mental pattern of the author, the personality realised in words. Style in poetry is partly a matter of rhythm; and rhythm, Dr Richards says very truly in *Science and Poetry*, 'is no matter of tricks with syllables, but directly reflects personality'. Mr Lewis would probably define style as the poet's credentials certifying him a person whom you can trust in the quest of bringing back true reports on the universe; and consider the report far more important than the credentials. But I should assert myself that experience shows how directly personality revealed through style can constitute the major appeal of poetry. It is pleasant to choose an example from a modern poet who considers poetry an escape from personality rather than an expression of it. In Mr T. S. Eliot's latest work, *The Rock*, the most successful passages are those where the author's characteristic rhythms and word-arrangements have freest scope, where his style is most obviously recognizable, in other words when he is most himself.

> *A Cry from the North, from the West and from the South:*
> *Whence thousands travel daily to the timekept City;*
> *Where My Word is unspoken,*
> *In the land of lobelias and tennis flannels*
> *The rabbit shall burrow and the thorn revisit,*
> *The nettle shall flourish on the gravel court,*

> *And the wind shall say: 'Here were decent godless*
> *people:*
> *Their only monument the asphalt road*
> *And a thousand lost golf balls.'*

Here the style *is* the poetry. The rhythm has a tense pregnant hush, simple in seeming, however subtle in the attainment, that sets off, that exploits to the utmost, the startling mixture of biblical reference and golf balls. It is entirely individual to the author, it reflects a poetical personality that quickens our pulses, and we value it far more than any heightened apprehension the passage may give us of the things of which it speaks. Mr Lewis might retort by attaching Mr Eliot, for all his professions of classicism, to the romantic tradition, and by pointing to his admission that for that tradition the personal theory does not work too badly. So I had better choose a second example not open to this retort; and I cannot do better in illustrating how widely I differ from Mr Lewis in my conception of the personal sphere in literature than choose the passage from Isaiah to which he refuses all personal quality whatsoever:

> And Babylon, the glory of kingdoms, the beauty of the Chaldees' excellency, shall be as

when God overthrew Sodom and Gomorrah. It shall never be inhabited, neither shall it be dwelt in from generation to generation: neither shall the Arabian pitch tent there: neither shall the shepherds make their fold there. But wild beasts of the desert shall lie there; and their houses shall be full of doleful creatures; and owls shall dwell there, and satyrs shall dance there. And the wild beasts of the islands shall cry in their desolate houses, and dragons in their pleasant palaces.

First, I am willing to admit with Mr Lewis that we do not through this passage get in touch with the personality of the original author, or at least, if we see him, it is at best through a mist. But with his remarks on the translator I disagree. Mr Lewis considers that he was so preoccupied with philological and theological matters that his own personality could find no entrance. This to my mind is to misunderstand not only translation but any art that appears to consist in getting a job of work done. Rule out the possibility of the translator mediating his own self, and you turn much early painting and sculpture, where the artist is fighting to render (as he thinks) a convincing likeness, into a mere technical exercise. On the contrary, it is precisely when a translator has worked himself up into an excited desire to do justice to a fine passage or a primitive sculptor is growing triumphant at surmounting a technical difficulty that his own mental pattern has the chance of manifesting itself. The artist will probably think his personality is lost in his non-personal activity, but the result may quite belie his own expectations. The sculptor of the Delphic Charioteer would have been incredulous if he had been told that his 'personality' had in any way entered into the figure of that impassive, severely draped young man; he probably thought he had done a good job of work and made a good imitation of the sort of driver who ought to win a chariot race for an illustrious prince. Yet the statue is like no other statue on earth, and I believe this unlikeness to be both an important element in the statue's excellence and to be connected with the sculptor's personality. Similarly the passage from Isaiah has a quite individual ferocity of rhythm which, if we heed it, will make the passage far less remote and romantic than Mr Lewis would have it be, and incidentally, not too far removed from the immediacy which he very justly postulates for the original. 'For us', says Mr Lewis, 'Babylon is far away and long ago': possibly, but was it so for a Protestant divine writing not long after the Gunpowder Plot? Not that the translator consciously or literally thought the passage a prophecy of the fall of the Papacy, and that he believed dragons would writhe in the ruined halls of the Vatican, but I suspect that Babylon evoked the Protestant fervour which was a motive in the translator's mental pattern. Of course a modern reader may let his mind be guided by the associations that the various evocative words in the passage have got for him: but this is rather an indulgence of the reader's own personal proclivities than a proper reading; 'personal' in a far less legitimate sense than in that of trying to establish contact with the mental pattern of the author.

When I spoke of the sculptor of the Delphic Charioteer having no notion that his own personality had anything to do with a statue, I was hinting at a paradox that may go a good way to explaining why people who may agree at bottom appear to think so differently about personality in literature. When Mr Eliot calls poetry 'an escape from personality', he means more than an escape from the accidents that attend a person in everyday life. He is trying to describe what it feels like when a man succeeds in writing poetry. The feeling (and other poets confirm Mr Eliot) brings with it the impression of a complete abandonment of personality, analogous to the feeling of 'getting out of yourself' that may occur in many non-literary contexts. Mr Eliot speaks of the poet 'surrendering himself wholly to the work to be done'. The paradox consists in the poet often producing the most characteristic and personal work through this very process of self-surrender. The more the poet experiences this abandonment of personality, the more likely is the reader to hail the poet's characteristic, unmistakable self. In fact the poet is *ipsissimus cum minime ipse*. Nor will it make the poet any less personal, if he carefully avoids every vestige of private emotion, if he seeks the utmost objectification. On the contrary, the pattern into which these apparently alien objects are fitted will express all the more clearly, with the least risk of encumbrance, the characteristic lines of the poet's mental pattern. Herein lies the reason why the following passage from Mr. Lewis's essay is no valid argument against the personal theory. In commenting on the lines from *Hyperion* he writes:

> It is absolutely essential that each word should suggest not what is private and personal to the poet but what is public, common, impersonal, objective. The common world with its nights, its oaks, and its stars, which we have all seen, and which mean at least *something* the same to all of us, is the bank on which he draws his cheques.

Here Mr Lewis is assuming that what is true of communication is true of the experience communicated. As far as the former goes, his doctrine is sound, containing the legitimate reproof of the kind of modern verse that draws its cheque on the banks of Albi or Florence or Timbuctoo rather than on the Bank of England. But as regards experience Mr Lewis is not always right. However public the means of communication, the experience conveyed may (among other things or even chiefly) be a mental pattern peculiar to the poet. Anyhow it is plain enough that those who choose to see only one half of the paradox will never agree with those who choose to see only the other.

However, granted the paradox, there remains another critical sense of the word *personal*. It is best set forth through Coleridge's comparison of Shakespeare and Milton in the fifteenth chapter of the *Biographia Literaria:*

> While the former darts himself forth, and passes into all the forms of human character and passion, the one Proteus of the fire and blood; the other attracts all forms and things to himself, into the unity of his own ideal. All things and modes of action shape themselves anew in the being of Milton; while Shakespeare becomes all things, yet forever remaining himself.

Now in a sense Shakespeare was just as thorough as Milton in impressing his own personality on the reader. But just because Shakespeare's own mental pattern largely consisted of an almost unexampled power of adapting itself to the shifting experiences of life so as to extract the utmost mental nourishment from them, his personality makes a much less precise effect on us than does the more rigid personality of Milton. When then we talk of the poetry of Milton or of Wordsworth being more personal than that of Shakespeare or of Keats we may be meaning that it expresses a more austerely rigid nature. Now these fluid and rigid natures, although they may both be transmuted into poetry and become thereby accessible, do react differently on the relation between the poet's life and the poet's art. The fluid, adaptable, receptive natures, granted power, are likely to be pure artists and to empty their lives for the sake of their art. Their power, their fierceness go to solving their artistic problems. Flaubert is habitually quoted as an author of this kind. The more rigid natures, who insist, for all their sensibility to impressions, on imposing their own very definite patterns on the world of their vision are likely to be interesting persons in their private lives, apt to do more notable things and to impress themselves on those around them. Thus Wordsworth must needs poke his nose into the French Revolution.

Before drawing some critical deductions from these statements, I wish to say that the above general division of authors into the fluid and empty-lived on the one hand, and the rigid and full-lived on the other, does not invalidate the analogy I postulated above between the mind-pattern as expressed in art and the mind-pattern as expressed in life. True, the analogy between a biography composed of a few dry facts supplemented by a few trivial anecdotes and a beautifully proportioned body of poetry can appear ridiculous. But it may be that the two versions differ less in kind than in completeness. One is a perfect volume; the other consists of a few mutilated pages. The mind-pattern is fully revealed in the poetry; from the biographical material its main lines are indecipherable. And yet the fact that we cannot decipher them does not prove that their trend is not similar to that purged, clarified, and intensified pattern that shows up in the poetry. Even when an author distils almost the whole of himself into his writing (as Flaubert did), what is left of the man, ghost-like and bloodless as it may be, can repeat in some vague sort the mental pattern that has been presented so perfectly in the works. Contact with him might inform us that here is a remarkable personality, but so abstracted from active living as to be unprofitable to pursue. In other words, even the author most depersonalized or sucked dry by his art is potentially a man of note outside the literary sphere.

Still, though the life of the man who has yielded himself to his art should present some analogy with that art, it may, however closely scrutinized, be entirely useless in heightening the appreciation of that art. In fact biographical study will in this case insist on staying on the hither side of criticism in the province of literary anecdotage. It is very likely that Shakespeare's biography, even with the fullest knowledge, would remain as at present in that province. But with the other class, the biography, the *facts* of personality, the data for the mental pattern of the man's life, may substantially help our understanding of the mental pattern as revealed in his art. An extreme example would be William Morris, a much less extreme one, Milton. And if, in writing of Milton, I have forsaken the safe Johnsonian example of not confounding biography and criticism, I would say in defence that I did so because I was writing of Milton, not because I thought they should invariably be so confounded. Yet I grant that the mixture of biography and criticism, even when most justified by the nature of the author, has its besetting danger: it is all too easy for the reader to use biography as an illegitimate short cut into the poet's mental pattern as revealed in his poems. He may arrive thereby at what seems a place higher up on the more difficult road of intensive study of the isolated word, but he will have missed the essential revelation that could only be obtained by the very journey he has shirked. He will, in fact, have been doing something like looking up the answers to a problem when tired of trying to solve it, or using a crib when reading a foreign text. It is when a man believes that the intensive study of the isolated word has gone astray or has been brought to a standstill that he is justified in seeking guidance from biography.

Mr Lewis's essay raises the whole question of what poetry is about. From the hints he drops I gather that for him poetry is about objects outside the poet's mind, about racial perception, and about God. My business is not with this topic, nor am I clear enough about Mr Lewis's views to be able to use them as a starting-point. But I wish to make two observations on it before I close. First, I disclaim any intention of limiting the value of poetry to establishing contact with an important personality; and I would refer the reader to an early chapter in my recent book, *Poetry Direct and Oblique,* in which I discuss the things poetry tends to concern. Some of these things, though we accept information about them only because we trust the person who gives it, are different from the personality or mental pattern of the author, described above. They are nearer, at any rate, to the discoveries about the universe that Mr Lewis expects the poet to make. Secondly, although I have departed from the doctrines of Dr Richards so far as to admit that the poet tells us things as well as imposes valuable equilibria on our minds, I find Mr Lewis too rigidly concerned with things and too little heedful of states of mind when he discusses his examples. My disagreement from him can best be illustrated by discussing one of his own instances, Herrick's *Upon Julia's Clothes*. Mr Lewis discusses half the poem. It may be fairer to take the whole:

> *Whenas in silks my Julia goes,*
> *Then, then, methinks, how sweetly flows*
> *That liquefaction of her clothes.*
> *Next, when I cast mine eyes, and see*
> *That brave vibration each way free;*
> *Oh, how that glittering taketh me!*

Commenting on the first three lines, Mr Lewis calls them 'poetry of an unusually sensuous and simple type', and says that in them 'the only experience which has any claim to be poetical experience is an apprehension not of the poet, but of silk'. The poet has presented an idea of silk and one of unusual vividness. Now Mr Lewis expressly excludes from the poetic value of the lines the notion, 'With what eyes the poet must have seen silk': that is merely an irrelevant afterthought. I can only conclude that in his opinion the lines concern not a state of mind but a substance called silk, and that they reveal hitherto unapprehended qualities of silk. What are these qualities? Mr Lewis suggests that the word *liquefaction* is responsible for the vividness with which silk is apprehended. In other words Herrick has made the discovery that compared with certain other textures (felt, for instance) silk resembles in its suppleness a liquid rather than a solid. I cannot believe that Mr Lewis really holds that the poem's virtue can reside in so elementary an observation, an observation in the power of so many people and not at all requiring the superior penetration of poetic genius. Yet what is the alternative? I can only see (granted silk as the concern of the poem) the vaguely mystical or Platonic notion (common enough in the late nineteenth century) that objects have some essential quality, some true self, which the artist can in some way reveal. Now such interpretations of poetry seem to me justified only if backed by the complete philosophy which they imply. Usually they imply no philosophy; and I doubt, from Mr Lewis's remarks, whether he really wishes to attach this particular poem to any comprehensive creed. If he does, I have no quarrel with him. If he does not, I think he has failed to attach any value to Herrick's lines.

What I cannot accept in Mr Lewis's interpretation of the poem is the value he puts on 'things'. I do not say that the poem does not tell us something, but I do say that what it tells us about silk has a very subordinate share in the poem's total meaning. Silk may have considerable importance as a means, as an end it is negligible. Even the claim of temporal priority made for silk (a claim whose importance I do not admit) is not justified; for before the silk is made vivid to us, we are given through the excited repetition of the words 'then, then', the statement of the speaker's excitement at the sight of his Julia in motion. Far from containing the virtue of the poem, the apprehension of silk is but one of a number of factors that go to express a state of mind which readers have somehow shared, and which they have considered in some way valuable. Here are a few of these factors. A fresh and unaffected sensuality pervades the poem. Not only is the speaker's excitement expressed by 'then, then', but from the flow of the clothes and their vibration the hint of the body beneath is not absent. The full emphasis and the fall of the third line express how well the spectator's excitement is satisfied by the downward flow of the silk. We may even derive from *liquefaction* a hint of the word *satisfaction*. *Liquefaction* is a sophisticated word, and as such is more important than as describing a quality of silk which (incidentally) had been already indicated in the word *flows*. More important, probably, than any of the factors noted above is the contrast on which the poem is constructed. The spectator first sees the downward flow of Julia's silks and he experiences satisfaction. He then sees the silks vibrating, perhaps moving in little horizontal eddies, and he is captivated. Even if this contrast means no more than a sense of balance or decorum it is not unimportant in the poem; and anyhow it is something very different from an isolated apprehension of silk.

Now few readers will accept all these observations on Herrick's poem, but I hope most of them will agree that it is complicated and not so very simple and sensuous. And I should be glad to think that they found it initially more reasonable to consider that poem in terms of a state of mind than in terms of a substance called silk. For it is not by any laborious process of induction *after* we have read the poem that we apprehend the qualities of unaffected sensuality, keen observation, sophistication, and sense of decorum. We apprehend them from the rhythm, the vocabulary, the word-arrangement, the pattern of the poem, in fact from the poem's most intimate poetical features. And the fact that such an enumeration is critically only of the most trivial value does not preclude its being on sounder lines than seeing the poem in terms of 'things'.

To go further, to describe the state of mind these qualities compose is luckily not necessary to my argument, nor need I reopen the question of how far it is the poet's personality we get in touch with through the poem. But I should like to add that seeing a poem in terms of a state of mind need not preclude 'Theism or Platonism or Absolute Idealism'. If you wish to see God in poetry, you can see Him as readily in the mind of a human being as in a piece of silk.

III

Id cinerem aut Manes credis curare sepultos?

Dear Dr Tillyard,
A friend of mine once described himself as being 'hungry for rational opposition'. The words seemed to me to hit off very happily the state of a man who has published doctrines which he knows to be controversial, and yet finds no one to voice the general disagreement that he looked for. It was with just such a hunger that I sat down to read your formidable *Rejoinder* to my essay on the *Personal Heresy*. In such matters to find an opponent is almost to find a friend; and I have to thank you very heartily for your kind and candid contribution to the problem.

In order to narrow the controversy as much as possible I will begin by recanting all that I can recant. If I have attributed any positions wrongly either to yourself or to Mr T. S. Eliot, I withdraw the attribution at once. My defence for choosing from your works and his what were, after all, but *obiter dicta,* is that my enemy was much less a fully fledged theory than a half-conscious assumption which I saw creeping into our critical tradition under the protection of its very vagueness. That I should choose my examples from the works of celebrated contemporaries was but reason. The heresy, if it be a heresy, which had deceived you, Sir, could not be regarded as contemptible. Nor do I defend my belief that this heresy is a new one. You may be right in considering it 'shop-soiled': and certainly our business is with its credentials, not its chronology. I will even give up my interpretation of the passage in Isaiah, and admit—if this seems to you to be the truth—that my reactions to it are private, partial, and idiosyncratic: that the good reader will find burning indignation where my romantic bias turned all 'to favour and to prettiness'. Whether my attack on the personal heresy is really a belittling of the individual or has any affinity with the 'totalitarian' position will best appear in what follows.

But while I gladly make these admissions, I cannot conceal the fact that there is a residuum of still unshaken disagreement; and to this I will now proceed. Your case against me, if I have read it aright, falls under four main heads. In the first place you meet my implied conception of personality with a *distinguo*. Personality, you point out, does not mean such trivial accidents as I suggest but rather 'some mental pattern which makes Keats Keats and not Mr Smith or Mr Jones',¹ and which you conceive as 'underlying the accidents of quotidian existence'² and displaying itself to us by style. In the second place you call my attention to what you describe as the 'Paradox' of poetic creation whereby the poet is *ipsissimus cum minime ipse*.³ Thirdly, you accuse me of confusing the means of communication with that which is communicated;⁴ and finally you are (in the old sense of the word) scandalized by my apparent preference of things to people.

You will observe that this list excludes some important passages in your *Rejoinder*, which I do not consider it my business to answer. I was much interested in your distinction between fluid and rigid personalities; but since, as you most candidly admit, the fluid cannot be 'deciphered' in their literary productions,⁵ their existence need not concern us at the moment, and if I can make good my case for the rigid I shall have made it good *a fortiori* for the fluid. Nor do I propose to make clear the supposed bases of my position in doctrines 'about racial perception, and about God'. To be sure, there is no denying that I consider my theory to be inconsistent with a thoroughgoing

---

¹ p. 42.
² p. 42.
³ p. 48.
⁴ p. 49.
⁵ p. 51.

materialism—like every other theory, including materialism itself. But I do not in the least wish to argue the matter on that level or postulate anything that would not be granted by 'common sense'—and if the conclusion of my essay has darkened counsel by awaking the uneasy theophobia of any of our contemporaries, I regret my blunder. I do not intend to relate my views to any 'vaguely mystical or Platonic notion (common enough in the late nineteenth century)'.[6] I will indeed confess that some desultory investigation of the problem of the Universal has left me with a certain respect for the solution (I would hardly call it vague) which Plato inclined to in the dialogues of his middle period; and my respect is not diminished by the popularity which Plato enjoyed in the nineteenth century any more than by that which he enjoyed in the seventeenth, sixteenth, fifteenth, third, second, or first. But I base nothing on Plato. If there is anything Platonic in my position, I trust I shall argue to it and act from it. There is, indeed, only one philosophical presupposition which I think I ought to make plain before I proceed. It is one with which you seem to disagree when you contrast the Personal with 'the abstract'.[7] You must excuse me, Sir, if I ask you

---

[6] p. 55.
[7] p. 38.

whether you really intend to identify the terms Personal and Concrete. If so, then the debate must indeed move on to quite different levels. I never intended to suggest that what poetry presented to us was the abstract; and I took it for granted that many things besides personality—things like apples—were concrete. Nay, if I thought personality the only concrete, I should also think it the 'subject of all verse': I should be a more radical 'personalist' than you. For me a person is neither less nor more concrete than a piece of silk (or felt!). Both are concrete, and of both it is fatally easy to think abstractly.

With this we reach the first main head—your contention that a just conception of personality can ignore trivial things, and rise above 'practical or everyday personality' to some 'mental pattern which makes Keats Keats', and which 'underlies' the 'accidents of quotidian existence'.[8] This doctrine has an old and honourable descent. Even without the word *underlie* (and its correlative *accidents*) it would be apparent that we have reached something very like the traditional definition of *substance:* and if we stress the distinction, implicit in your language, between the superior dignity of the true personality and the 'triviality' of its 'quotidian' 'accidents', we shall find ourselves

---

[8] p. 42.

in agreement with that doctrine of the Noumenal and Phenomenal selves which some would call vague and mystical and which was certainly popular in the nineteenth century. For my own part, Sir, I have not the least objection to finding myself on the same side as Kant, or even the Schoolmen, in a matter of logic. But while I am anxious to exclude personality from what I believe to be its wrong place, I am much too fond of personality in its right place to accept this purified, underlying, expurgated version of it. The thing may exist (or subsist?) in some hyperuranian realm: but is it what we mean by personality? 'Nothing', said Johnson, 'is too little for so little a creature as man'; and I submit that beings purged, as you suggest, of all that is little, would not be men. The smell of boiled beef, and presumably Keats's reactions to the smell, you exclude from 'that which makes him Keats'. What, then, of wine and his reaction to wine? Must the blushful Hippocrene be left behind with the beef, or have drinks some privilege of soaring into the realms that food cannot enter? What of women, whom Keats confessedly classed with confectionery? Do they drag up the sweetmeats to the Noumenal, or do the sweetmeats keep them down to the Phenomenal? In a word, what resemblance would your very Keats bear to the man who wrote the poems and is now dead? Take a man's mistress, or his daughter, and give her back to him attenuated to some such 'mental pattern', so freed from trivialities, and he will exclaim that he might as well have followed her coffin to the grave. 'Personality', in the sense suggested, is not the object of affection: it is not the subject of legal rights or moral obligations: it has not, since the pattern changes, the continuity claimed for the 'soul' in other systems: in a word it does not seem to me to deserve the name 'personality' in any respect. A man whom I know dreamed that he was at Falstaff's funeral; and as the mourners were saying that they had lost only the mortal husk of Sir John and that the real man awaited them in a better world, my friend awoke crying out, 'But we've lost his *fatness*!' I am not sure about the theology of this, but I approve the sentiment. Where personality is in question I will not give up a wrinkle or a stammer. I am offended when a man whom I heartily love or hate starts wearing a new kind of hat.

It may be replied that this is a dispute about a word. If you choose to call this purged 'mental pattern' by the name of Personality, why should I protest? I think, Sir, for a good reason. The name suggests warmth and humanity, intimacy, the real rough and tumble of human life: it is by that suggestion that the personal heresy gains adherents. Would any one have embraced it—would you yourself, Sir, have embarked on its defence—if it were clear from the outset that the only personality in question was personal in so very Pickwickian a sense? But I will not press the point. Let us suppose that such 'mental patterns' exist, and that they are properly called personalities. The question still remains whether our apprehension of them is valuable because they are such and such patterns, or because the things seen through them are interesting or valuable. I do not think the discussion has left that question just where it found it. When once such mental patterns have been detached from the quotidian selves which they underlie, what other value can they possibly have than the value I suggest—that of being glasses or windows through which we see what is worth seeing? For certainly you can no longer talk with them, fight with them, drink with them, or *dele drwry*.

Let us turn to the second point—the paradox of art, whereby the artist never expresses himself so clearly as when he has suppressed his personality. You will remember that you illustrated this doctrine by a reference to the Delphic Charioteer. The sculptor, you assumed, had no thought of self-expression: 'yet' (you continue) 'the statue is like no other statue on earth'.[9] What then? I never dreamed of denying that a great work of art was unique.

---

[9] p. 46.

That, Sir, is not the question between us. The question is whether the experience which we have of such uniqueness is an experience of the artist's personality: or, more simply, whether a great (and therefore, doubtless, a unique) work expresses the maker. This being so, to argue 'The statue is unlike all others: therefore it has expressed the sculptor's personality' would be a glaring *petitio*, and one which you have abstained from. (Your sentence runs on: 'I *believe* this unlikeness . . . to be *connected with* the sculptor's personality.')[10] But then it is not easy to see how the Delphic Charioteer will help us. Doubtless he is unique, *sui generis*, unpredictable and irrepeatable; but how can we thence infer the personality of the carver when it is clear that other things—things which are not works of art at all—are equally unique? It is not only poems or statues which seem to say, 'I am myself alone'. A sunset, a flight of birds past the window, the gesture of an athlete, or the sudden onset of rain—any of these, at a favoured moment, may come over us with just that sense of unity and individuality which you describe and extort from us a *verweile doch*. It need not even be a 'thing', in any ordinary sense, that produces this experience: it is often a contingent bundle of the most heterogeneous data. The

---

[10] p. 46.

sun comes out—a cock crows in the yard—at the same moment I finish reading the *Orlando Furioso* for the first time; and all this becomes for me a unique whole, memorable and unified as a sonata, singular and definite in flavour as a sonnet, an apple, or a kiss. I am sure I should be answered pretty quickly if I tried to argue directly from such experiences to some highly personal form of theism; but my inference would be neither more nor less valid than that from the felt individuality of a statue to the belief that we are apprehending the personality of a sculptor. It is true, of course, that we start by knowing that a man made the statue as we do not start by knowing that a god made my sun-cockcrow-Ariosto complex. But does this really help? The experience occurs both when there is no known artist in question and when there is. It is simply bad logic to devise for one phenomenon an explanation that will not cover the other. If we allowed the artist's personality to cover the instance of the charioteer, we should still have the sunsets on our hands, and when we had found a new explanation for them (theological, daemonological, psychoanalytical, physiological, or what not) then, clearly, this new explanation could be used to cover the charioteer as well, and by the law of Occam's razor ought to be so used. The first hypothesis would now be otiose—an *entitas ficta praeter necessitatem*.

I cannot help thinking that the common, but invalid, inference from the uniqueness of the work to the personality of the worker is an unconscious pun. When we claim individuality for the statue, we are using the word in its philosophical sense. Every concrete, everything that occupies space or time or both, is in this sense an individual: and it is the privilege of art (as also, more mysteriously, of certain moments outside art) to make us vividly aware of the fact. But when we pass from this real individuality in the work to a belief that we are in contact with a personality, are we not possibly misled by the fact that the word *individual* has another meaning in colloquial language? Because the work is individual we conclude that it displays to us 'an individual' in the popular sense—that is, a mind or soul or person.

To you, Sir, it seems that I am choosing to see only one half of the paradox[11]—viz. the artist's self-suppression. I reply that the other half of the paradox (his self-expression) can be granted only if we are already agreed that great and unique work expresses personality. But this, unfortunately, is the very thing we are debating.

The third charge against me is that I have confused communication with the thing communicated. You hold

---

[11] p. 49.

that my analysis of the lines from *Hyperion*, while it may show that the instruments which Keats uses are common and impersonal, by no means shows that the same is true of the experience which he records. But then this analysis was meant to show only the one, and not the other. Having established, as I thought, the impersonality of the means, I then proceeded[12] to work out an independent proof of the impersonality of the content: in the form, what's more, of a dilemma with two horns and everything handsome about it. Since you, Sir, have not here perfectly followed my argument, I have little doubt that the passage is culpably obscure; and I am confirmed in this unwelcome conclusion by the fact that I am now approaching a part of the question which has certainly been darkened by my carelessness.

You find me 'too rigidly concerned with things and too little heedful of states of mind'.[13] You cannot understand 'the value I put on "things"'.[14] You have the impression that silk, or even felt, interest me more than the fair bodies or wise heads which they adorn. The impression is false—but I have only myself to blame. What follows must be taken as words spoken from the stool of penance.

---

[12] p. 26.
[13] p. 54.
[14] p. 56.

When I talked of 'things' I meant to contrast them not with 'people' in general but with that particular person whom we call the poet. Silk was preferred not to Julia, but to Herrick: trees not to Saturn and Thea, but to Keats. In fact, I was including 'people' as a species of 'things'—though how I supposed that the reader would divine this is not easy to see. Let me now make a fresh start: and if it prove a better one, I shall owe it all to you. I freely admit that the 'things' most commonly presented to us in great literature are precisely those highly specialized things which we call men and women. To think of literature is to think first and foremost not of silks or forests but of Patroclus or Sancho Panza, of Roland or Micawber or Macbeth. When I selected the silk from Herrick's poem, I did so merely for the sake of simplicity. If I had dealt with the whole poem, with Julia-in-silk, the result would have been just the same. To me, the end attained by reading the poem is a heightened perception of the charm of a beautiful woman beautifully dressed. Now I admit that this charm is conveyed to me by an account of the effect which it had (or is feigned to have had) on Herrick. But, to speak the bare truth, it never occurred to me before I read your rejoinder that either the poet or any of his readers was in the least interested in this effect at all except in so far as it is the necessary medium through which its cause (the attractiveness of Julia) appears. Let us suppose for the moment that the poem is autobiographical. Surely you will grant that Herrick, in the article of his love-liking, was interested in Julia, not in his own reactions to Julia—nay, those reactions *consisted in* the fact that Julia, not Herrick, absorbed him. To attend to Herrick, therefore, is to cut ourselves off from the experience that Herrick is trying to convey. To be sure, the epistemologists will tell us that Julia's attractiveness is not a quality inherent in Julia but an effect she produces on observers. But unhappily they will tell us the same of her colour, warmth, fragrance, softness—and even, in a sense, of her size. But certainly poetry can make nothing of this way of thinking. Poetry, like unreflective experience, must attribute not only secondary but even tertiary qualities to the object: it must give the green to the tree not to our eyes, the scent to the flowers not to our noses, the attractiveness to the woman not to our sexual nature. Julia can be described in poetry, only by her effects; but the same holds (in poetry) of sun and moon and God Almighty. Herrick has awakened to the miracle that Julia is: but it is the miracle, not the fact of his awakening, that interests both him and us—though, admittedly, we should not be interested unless he had so awaked.

The same desire for simplicity which confused my treatment of Herrick's poem led me, in general, to illustrate my position by passages of natural description. I see now that this has inevitably made it appear that I set some peculiar value on the inanimate. But I do not. Among the objects presented to us by imaginative literature, people or 'personalities' hold the chief place. I wish to exclude none of them—only the poet himself. I want all the people whom Shakespeare invented; but not Shakespeare. And the reason for this seemingly fantastic distinction is really a very simple one.

But before I proceed to state it, I would remind you that I am theorizing not about art in general but about literature; and not even about all literature, but about imaginative literature—about poetry, drama, and the novel. I am prepared to grant that there are writings, and writings properly called literature, whose value consists in the impression they give us of the writer's personality. Private letters are obviously in this class: and many essays are also in it. I should not be greatly disturbed if we found, now and then, a piece of such writing which, by a 'sport', had put on the disguise of verse. Nor do I deny that there are borderline cases—things which might plausibly be reckoned either as imaginative literature or as instances of that truly personal writing which is but talking at a distance. The distinctions between animal and vegetable or day and night remain just and profitable although they are blurred at the frontiers. And within the realm of imaginative literature there is, I maintain, a good reason for putting the poet out of sight while we read.

It is sometimes asked whether Shakespeare was like this or that character in his plays. I do not know the answer. But there is one difference between Shakespeare and all his characters which I do know. Shakespeare was a real person: they are all imaginary people. When I read the plays I prepare myself for *feigning*—they do but jest, poison in jest. My objection to the poet's personality is that it is an intruder in this imagined world—an intruder, I may add, from a much higher realm—and that his presence amidst his own creations, if it occurred, would demand from me, at the same moment, two incompatible responses. For Shakespeare was a real man. My response to the real both is and ought to be quite distinct from my response to the imaginary. Every child knows that we do well to watch, and, in a sense, to enjoy, the murder of Desdemona; and every child knows that if we so watched and so enjoyed the like in real life, we should be villains.

You, Sir, have said that 'part of our response to poetry is similar to the stirring we experience when we meet some one whose personality impresses us'.[15] It is indeed.

---

[15] p. 42.

The greatest of all similarities exists between a face and that face reflected in a mirror, between a body and a shadow, between a thing and the same thing imagined. Long ago Hume found how hard it is to define the difference between an 'idea' and an 'impression'. But are we therefore to identify them? Does any one doubt that this similarity is consistent with the most important of all differences? And if so, how can I offer to the poet the same response which I offer to his poetry? The poet is a man, a real man. I exclude him not because I think meanly of personality but because I reverence it. There is something to make the blood run cold in the very idea of offering to a man, even to a dead man like Keats, that same 'willing suspension of disbelief', that impartial, unhelping, uninterfering, acquiescent contemplation which I offer to Hyperion or Enceladus. The poet is my fellow creature—a traveller between birth and death—one of *us*. My response to him is not on the plane of imagination at all. The appeal of real personality is to the heart—to the will and the affections. The proper pleasure of it is called love, the proper pain, hatred. I do not owe the poet some aesthetic response: I owe him love, thanks, assistance, justice, charity—or, it may be, a sound thrashing.

The last alternative is important. When the personality of the poet happens to be one we like, there is some excuse for confusing imaginative delight in the work with social or affectional delight in the man. But what of the poets whose personality we dislike? There is a strong personality in Dryden, and I happen to dislike it very much. But I delight in the *boisterousness* and bravura of his scenes, as in the sweetness of his verse. Am I wrong to disregard the personal antipathy while I read, in order to enjoy the poetry? If you say that I ought to correct the antipathy, then you lift me at once out of the imaginative into the ethical. For to decide that question we must start investigating historical data and moral principles, and *Absalom and Achitophel* meanwhile will have to wait. It is the very nature of a real personality, once seriously considered, to force us out of the world of poetry.

Perhaps this is best seen when we are dealing with a contemporary poet. Your quotation from Mr Eliot here comes to hand. We are in some disagreement about its merits—I would not call the mixture of golf balls and biblical reference 'startling',[16] and would scarcely have called it startling ten years ago—but it is certainly good enough for our purpose. Now to read these lines as poetry surely means to see the 'land of lobelias and tennis flannels', suspending (if need be) my disbelief, and to derive from that

---

[16] p. 44.

vision such pleasure or profit as I may. To attempt this is my debt to Mr Eliot's poetry. And if, instead, I surrender myself to the 'feel' of Mr Eliot's personality (as indeed I easily can), if I allow myself to attend to the kind of man thus speaking of the suburbs, then I find myself carried into realms of thought and feeling which are fatal to the reception of poetry. For Mr Eliot, thus dismissing some tens of thousands of my fellow citizens, is something even more important than a poet. He is a man: and, being a widely influential man, he is either friend or foe—either a *vox clamantis* at which I should tremble, or a proud, misunderstanding detractor whom I should strive to silence, if I can, and then pardon. And this not only happens to me but happens with my approval. Mr Eliot is my fellow creature: those whose necessities make them live in the suburbs are also my fellow creatures. When I think of him (which in this context involves thinking of them too) I not only am carried, but ought to be carried, out of poetic attention into that larger world where literary laws must yield to laws logical and ethical.

I hope it is now apparent that my doctrine depends as much on my respect for men as on my respect for things. If I regard Mr Eliot as a friend, well. If I regard him as an enemy, then by so doing I honour his personality much more than by treating him as a doll or a picture, or an object of contemplation. I will try another dilemma. You maintain that we do well to respond to the poet's personality while we read. But if this is the response really proper to personality—the practical, affective response of love or hatred made by one man to another—then it overwhelms poetry in matters more important, though poetically irrelevant. If it is anything less than this, if it is some purely contemplative, appraising, criticizing gaze, then it is an insult. It is to make of a man a mere thing, a spectacle. We do not wish to be thus treated ourselves. Is there, in social life, a grosser incivility than that of thinking about the man who addresses us instead of thinking about what he says? For my own part, I feel that I should use a dog rather ill if I regarded it with that detached observation which we accord to Hamlet and Imogen.

But there is yet another way in which the personal heresy offends against personality; and it is one which all members of our profession must ponder. I am referring to the growth of what may be called Poetolatry. Some time ago Matthew Arnold prophesied that poetry would come to replace religion; and the personal heretics have made this true in a sense which he probably did not foresee. Poetry has, naturally enough, not yet attempted the salvation of souls or the enlightenment of the understanding; but the cult of poetry is taking on some secondary religious characteristics—notably the worship of saints and the traffic in relics. Every teacher of English has had pupils to whom the study of literature principally meant a series of acts of devotion to various dead men who wrote poetry. We have biographies of Keats and even (I believe) of D. H. Lawrence which are almost exercises in hagiography. We have even had such tangled trinities as 'Christ, Shakespeare, and Keats' proposed to us. If we have also our 'debunking' biographies, that is but the reverse side of the same medal: blasphemy is the child of religion. I have no doubt, Sir, that you agree with me, simply as a man of letters and a teacher, in lamenting this collapse from criticism into cult. But there are deeper reasons for condemning it. If personality is among the noblest modes of being, as you and I believe, then it is important that our response to personality should not be side-tracked or perverted. And that response is essentially a social and affective one. It is called love—whether ἔρως, θιλία, or στοργή. As there is no other way of enjoying beer but by drinking it, or of enjoying colour but by looking at it, so there is no other way of enjoying personality but by loving it. For veneration, pity, and the like are species of love.

Now it is clearly not desirable that too much of this response should, in any event, be directed towards the dead. But when the dead are really lovable and loved by us for that reason, this extension of our affective life into the past is not unnatural. The recorded personalities of Socrates, Johnson, and Scott compel such affection. Our love of them is an extension, not a misdirection, of the impulse: the object, though distant and unresponsive, is still a personality in the full sense, with all its quotidian trivialities about it. But the case is altered if we are dealing with that 'mental pattern' which exists in a good book, and specially in a good poem. The nobility of Johnson is a real thing, and so is the nobility of the *Aeneid;* but the nobility of Virgil is a mere snare for self-deception, because we can (within very wide limits indeed) fashion that idol any shape we want. Johnson, because his personality survives—because he affects us as a man and not merely as an author—is obstinate and resistant. We converse with him, being men ourselves, under 'the mutual awe of equal condition'. Virgil is malleable: he will never pull you up short, as Johnson, even across the centuries, so often does. It is no good pretending that Johnson would have listened sympathetically to an account of my repressions: it is quite easy (if one likes) to imagine Virgil doing so. The excellence of Donne's pornographic elegies is a fact: so is the excellence of his devotional poetry. But the 'personality' constructed to explain their coexistence (as if it needed any explanation!) may well be a mere projection on which modern adolescents can lavish any kind of familiarity they choose. The real absurdity of the triad I mentioned above—Christ, Shakespeare, and Keats—lies in the heterogeneity of its members. From the Christian point of view there are other objections; but for my present purpose it is enough to notice that while the first member exists for us as a man, even as Johnson exists, the second does not exist at all, and the third only to a limited degree. The injunction to obey Christ has a meaning: the injunction to obey Shakespeare is meaningless. Attention to Shakespeare's 'personality' can have no influence on any human action: it is a misdirection of feelings properly social and active to an object which admits of no action and no true society.

There is a reaction at present going on against the excessive love of pet animals. We have been taught to despise the rich, barren woman who loves her lap-dog too much and her neighbour too little. It may be that when once the true impulse is inhibited, a dead poet is a nobler substitute than a live Peke, but this is by no means obvious. You can do something for the Peke, and it can make some response to you. It is at least sentient; but most poetolaters hold that a dead man has no consciousness, and few indeed suppose that he has any which we are likely to modify. Unless you hold beliefs which enable you to obey the colophons of the old books by praying for the authors' souls, there is nothing that you can do for a dead poet: and certainly he will do nothing for you. He did all he could for you while he lived: nothing more will ever come. I do not say that a personal emotion towards the author will not sometimes arise spontaneously while we read; but if it does we should let it pass swiftly over the mind like a ripple that leaves no trace. If we retain it we are but cosseting with substitutes an emotion whose true object is our neighbour. Hence it is not surprising that those who most amuse themselves with personality after this ghostly fashion often show little respect for it in their parents, their servants, or their wives. You, Sir, know far more psychology than I. There is no need for me to tell you how such substitutions work upon a man; how such facile satisfactions of a vital impulse, allayings spun from our own inwards and therefore never inaccessible, never resistant, never to be paid for in cash, disable and (as it were) drive out of the market that difficult and fruitful obedience to the same impulse which can be learnt only in the real world. For the sake of personality, therefore, we must reject the personal heresy. We must go to books for that which books can give us—to be interested, delighted, or amused, to be made merry or to be made wise. But for the proper pleasure of personality, that is, for love, we must go where it can be found—to our homes or our common rooms, to railway carriages and public houses, or even (for you see I am one of the vulgar) to the 'land of lobelias and tennis flannels'.

And with this, my case is ended. As I glance through the letter again I notice that I have not been able, in the heat of argument, to express as clearly or continuously as I could have wished my sense that I am engaged with 'an older and a better soldier'. But I have little fear that you will misunderstand me. We have both learnt our dialectic in the rough academic arena where knocks that would frighten the London literary coteries are given and taken in good part; and even where you may think me something too pert you will not suspect me of malice. If you honour me with a reply it will be in kind; and then, God defend the right!

I am, my dear Sir, with the greatest respect,
    Your obedient servant,
    C. S. Lewis.

IV

In my *Rejoinder* I said that I agreed with a good deal of what Mr Lewis said. From his *Open Letter* it is clear to me that our positions are beginning to approximate and that controversy has been fulfilling one of its proper functions: that of clearing away misconceptions. With some people it is a pleasure to differ, and total agreement must always be dull; but I should be seriously perturbed if I found myself utterly opposed to Mr Lewis, for whose work I have so high a regard. Anyhow, my present task will partly consist in showing how I agree with Mr Lewis in spite of appearances to the contrary. After that I may be able to narrow the field of dispute still further and restate my position. Whether Mr Lewis will accept that position as restated, I do not know. If he does not, I think our differences will have been sufficiently defined to make further discussion superfluous. On the other hand, I am anxious to tempt Mr Lewis to prolong the argument in another direction.

First, let us get rid of a few details. I certainly never meant, when I spoke of a modern tendency to 'belittle the personal in comparison with the abstract, the Renaissance in comparison with Byzantium', to insinuate that the *personal* was the only *concrete*. The word *abstract* was badly chosen; substitute, if you will, *impersonal* (but this is very weak), or *ideal* (but this may also be ambiguous).

Secondly, we are still at cross-purposes over Herrick's Julia poem. When I charged Mr Lewis with being 'too rigidly concerned with things and too little heedful of states of mind', I didn't mean that I thought him oblivious of Julia, and I was quite aware that Julia was among those things a too rigid concern with which I deprecated. But, Mr Lewis having spoken of silk, I found it more emphatic to follow his lead and to stick to silk as typifying all the external objects which poetry is free to describe. What I meant was that I sometimes find that the criticism which tries to explain the author's state of mind instead of talking about the counters used in the poem ('things') gives me satisfaction. And I suggested that a certain detail of form, indicating a state of mind in the poet, a sense of balance or decorum, was, in the poem under review, important. That the poet when he writes poetry does not put his reactions in subjective terms I of course agree ('Poetry', says Mr Lewis, 'must give the green to the tree and not to our eyes'); but this does not prove that the poet's main concern is not a state of mind or that Julia and her clothes ('things' or 'counters' as I deliberately called them) are *necessar-*

ily more than vehicles for some emotion not usually or at first sight attached to them. 'Herrick', says Mr. Lewis, 'has awakened to the miracle that Julia is; but it is the miracle, not the fact of his awakening, that interests both him and us.' That is possible, but there is no *a priori* impossibility in Julia being, rather, one of several convenient symbols contributing to express the sense of order or decorum the poet is primarily expressing. My point will be clearer if I turn from Herrick's Julia to Marvell's Juliana.

The Mower to the Glow-worms.

Ye living lamps, by whose dear light
   The nightingale does sit so late,
And studying all the summer night,
   Her matchless songs does meditate;

Ye country comets, that portend
   No war nor prince's funeral,
Shining unto no higher end
   Than to presage the grass's fall;

Ye glow-worms, whose officious flame
   To wandering mowers shows the way,
That in the night have lost their aim,
   And after foolish fires do stray;

Your courteous lights in vain you waste,
Since Juliana here is come;
For she my mind hath so displaced
That I shall never find my home.

To one passage at least of this poem Mr Lewis's way of approach seems to me appropriate; that is to the glow-worms presaging the fall of the grass. The poet's genius does indeed seem to heighten our apprehension of the literal fact that the glow-worms or fire-flies haunt the fully ripe hay fields. And because I find Mr Lewis's method so appropriate here, I care the less whether or not I find it 'true'. But what of the nightingales? Does the fancy of the bird reading the score of an air by the light of the glow-worms' midnight oil in the least heighten our apprehension of the actual nightingale's song? I cannot think it. Even if you disagree with me, what of the third verse? The picture of an agricultural labourer saved from will-o'-the-wisps by the kindly solicitude of the glow-worms cannot by any mental effort be made to help us appreciate rural life more intensely; on the contrary it queers that particular appreciation. And what finally of Juliana? Herrick's Julia and her dress may well be related to actuality. Juliana is clearly no more than a convenience for pulling the poem's shape together: nearer allied to a corset than to a woman. This being so, I fail to see how it does much good to discuss the complete poem and most of its details in terms of 'things'. The more profitable method is to be more personal, to discuss the poem in terms of the poet's feelings, to involve oneself, in fact, in the personal heresy.

I must now turn from dispute to rehearsing a list of apologies due to Mr Lewis. I admit that my accusing him of seeing only one-half of a certain paradox amounted to no more than accusing him of not agreeing with me on the main point at issue. I withdraw my charge that in speaking of *Hyperion* he confused communication with the thing communicated. And I plead guilty of vagueness when citing the 'unlikeness' of the Delphic Charioteer to any other statue and the connexion of that unlikeness or uniqueness with the sculptor's personality. But I do not surrender what I had in mind, however imperfectly put on paper, to the formidable battery of Mr Lewis's dialectic. To this uniqueness I will turn, but not before thanking Mr Lewis for his keen probings, some of which have revealed what was unsound, others helped me to mend my thoughts.

Mr Lewis objects to my connecting the uniqueness of the Delphic Charioteer with the sculptor's personality on the ground that this very sense of uniqueness can be felt in apprehending 'a sunset, a flight of birds past the window, the gesture of an athlete, or the sudden onset of rain', none of which are works of art. 'The experience occurs both when there is no known artist and when there is.' Personality cannot account for all the instances. What reason then for allowing it to account for the uniqueness of the Charioteer? The argument is good, but I dispute the premises. I do not in fact allow to all the phenomena under review (pardon the phrase) the same quality of uniqueness. They are indeed phenomena of different kinds which we should expect a person to enjoy in different ways. We may legitimately couple the sunset and the rain. I don't mind including with them the birds, although I would remind Mr Lewis that we have it on the authority of one who was both poet and scientist that

> *Birds are of all animals the nearest to men*
> *for that they take delight in both music and dance,*
> *and gracefully schooling leisure to enliven life*
> *wer the earlier artists.*

But the gesture of an athlete I cannot allow in the list unless it is more narrowly defined; because such a gesture, if the result of long training and much joy, may be allied to the mimetic dance, may be indistinguishable from a work of art; to be classed with the Delphic Charioteer. Anyhow I postulate at least two classes for the things or acts Mr Lewis enumerates; and correspondingly in enjoying them we get different sensations. And it remains to be seen whether the sense of uniqueness we talk of is single or follows the different sensations proper to each class.

Trying to recapture and analyze any feelings I have had in the matter, I differ from Mr Lewis in that I find this sense of uniqueness to be a rough account of more than one state of mind. It may imply in the main that here is something very well worth our attention, something we must on no account miss. A natural consequence of such a thought is that perhaps the present chance of enjoyment may not recur; so quite easily, though truncatedly, we sum up the *whole* process by expressing the last phase alone — the improbability of recurrence — using some word like *unique*. Secondly, there is Mr Lewis's use, which he describes too well for me not to use his words. He says of the sunset, the flight of birds, &c., that

> any of these, at a favoured moment, may come over us with just that sense of unity and individuality which you describe and extort from us a *verweile doch*.

The last phrase implies pretty much what I have just described. But the 'sense of unity' is surely another and separate sensation. We may witness many events or objects and think them unique without having any sense of unity: such as a royal funeral, or our first play, or Etna in eruption. If mere interest reaches a certain pitch we attribute uniqueness to those experiences. But a sense of unity is of a different order, allying us however distantly to the poet and the mystic. And if we describe this sense of unity as *unique,* as we may easily do, it is, as I said, a very rough and inadequate account indeed.

Now both these meanings of unique can be applied to all the objects (the Delphic Charioteer included) enumerated by Mr Lewis. But, culpable as I was in applying so vague a word as *unlikeness* (for which I would quite readily have used *uniqueness* instead) to the effect produced by that statue, I did not mean by it either of the two qualities above described. But I did mean something both different from them and inapplicable to sunsets and showers. What I said fumblingly about the Charioteer was said much better (naturally) by Jane Austen in answering a letter from her niece:

> You are so odd, and all the time so perfectly natural! so peculiar in yourself, and yet so like everybody else!

The sensation of unlikeness, or uniqueness, is here combined with that of kinship and recognition. Jane Austen at once feels her niece very alien and yet recognizes herself and all women in her. Similarly, in spite of its apparent remoteness, its solitary existence in a strange and antique world, the Delphic Charioteer can awaken the sense of kinship and of sharing. And this paradox is so striking that the experience stands out as exceedingly interesting and significant; and we are again tempted to call it unique. I fancy that some such experience is described by Longinus when in his seventh chapter of *On the Sublime* he says,

> For, as if instinctively, our soul is uplifted by the true sublime; it takes a proud flight, and is filled with joy and vaunting, *as though it had itself produced what it has heard.*

The above may give some notion of the feelings I had in mind when I spoke of the 'unlikeness' of the Delphic Charioteer to any other work of art. I do not wish to imply that the feelings Mr Lewis attaches to *unique* may not apply also, or that 'personality' is the only ground of appeal possessed by the statue. And now, having opened the question of sharing or recognition, I will say something more of it in general.

It is highly probable that in matters of literary criticism our own mental temper dictates both the kind of things we say and the satisfaction we get from this or that way of speaking by others. And no amount of argument will alter such a dictation. This does not mean that one person cannot profit by the opinions of another; but it may mean that frank personal testimony is often more profitable than argument, because the latter can so easily be but the personal bent pretending to a ridiculously unjustified universality. I should therefore like to interpose a very simple piece of testimony, presenting it as apparent experience and as nothing more.

Adequate enjoyment of works of art seems to depend on chance. We happen, we cannot guess why, to be in the right mood; and the obstacles usually interposed between us and the artistic object disappear. By some chance the obstacles chose to remove themselves when I was surveying one (and probably not the best) of a number of romanesque churches I was in the course of visiting in the Auvergne. Among other feelings experienced there presented itself to me with considerable emphasis and apparent spontaneity the one that I was sharing something with the man who had designed the church. The feeling seemed not particularly different in quality from that intimacy that can subsist or can be imagined to subsist in ordinary life between lovers or other people united in uncommon sympathy. It was certainly very different in circumstances, because I had no idea who the architect was or even whether he was known. Nor did I feel the least curiosity to find out. All that matters to me is that the feeling referred to appeared both personal and valuable.

Mr Lewis is free to be utterly sceptical of the truth of the above personal impression and to think me gravely deluded. On the other hand, the episode may reassure him that I refrain from those grosser confoundings of the feelings proper to art with those proper to life which he so eloquently describes and condemns. With most of that condemnation I heartily agree. Yet I believe that he presses the distinction between art and life too far. To treat a dead artist with the social technique proper to dealing with a generous employer, a troublesome neighbour, or an admired parliamentary candidate is a wild abuse. Yet I would maintain that my relations with the Auvergne architect were free from that abuse, yet personal; outside the sphere of action, yet of a kind to be found in ordinary life. Which brings me to another of Mr Lewis's dilemmas:

> You maintain that we do well to respond to the
> poet's personality while we read. But if this is
> the response really proper to personality—the

practical, affective response of love or hatred made by one man to another—then it overwhelms poetry in matters more important, though poetically irrelevant. If it is anything less than this, if it is some surely contemplative, appraising, criticizing gaze, then it is a mere insult.

To this I reply that though the 'practical, affective response of love or hatred made by one man to another' may be the usual rule of human relations, it is not invariably so. There are times of sympathy between human beings when anything 'practical' is as grossly inappropriate as 'a willing suspension of disbelief' would be towards a man with a broken leg calling for first aid. Normally, such times of sympathy are arrived at through familiarity and much practical traffic. Nevertheless that tragic is irrelevant to the moment when it comes. Moreover, the experience can occur between comparative strangers, between people of widely different natures, to whom the normal familiarities would be impossible. It certainly occurred in the late War, and is likely to occur at any crisis. The experience is personal in the sense under review because it cannot happen to a man alone and consists largely in the act of sharing; yet it reduces the sharers, and that without insult and inappropriateness, to all the stripping of personality their natures can bear.

One of the results of any successful sharing of this sort is a heightened sensibility. If I look at a sunset or a cloud that's dragonish with a sympathetic companion, and we are successful in sharing the experience, I am likely to see the scene with keener eyes. Mr Lewis would have it that good sunset-gazing mainly concerns the sunset alone; I, on the other hand, distinguish between solitary gazing and gazing in company. In both acts there will be a heightened apprehension; and both will be good, but not in the same way. That the act in company is likely to be a ticklish business does not shut out its few successful consummations. And these, as well as other feelings, contain some that have to do with companionship—feelings for instance of the common lot of man in good and ill, or of the mysterious truth that the enisled beings can at times at least imagine themselves part of the single continent—and their force is conditioned by, is inseparable from, the flow of sympathy to and from the other person.

In describing this experience in life I have been simultaneously pointing to one value of personality in literature. One immediately apparent difference can quickly be explained. A flow of sympathy backwards and forwards is conceivable in life; how is it possible in art, between a dead writer and a living reader? I reply that all expression in a medium comprehensible to a public constitutes in itself an invitation at least to share, sometimes to sympathize. Even a riddle has little point if it is too difficult ever to admit a solver. It may invite a very select company but invite it does.

From the poet's point of view Wordsworth expresses this notion of *sharing* in the section of his Preface to the Lyrical Ballads, *What Is a Poet?* The poet himself is

> a man speaking to men; a man . . . endowed with more lively sensibility, more enthusiasm and tenderness, who has a greater knowledge of human nature, and a more comprehensive soul, than are supposed to be common among mankind. . . . The knowledge both of the Poet and the Man of science is pleasure; but the knowledge of the one cleaves to us as a necessary part of our existence, our natural and unalienable inheritance; the other is a personal and individual acquisition, slow to come to us, and by no habitual and direct sympathy connecting us with our fellow-beings. . . . The Man of science seeks truth as a remote and unknown benefactor; he cherishes and loves it in solitude: the

Poet, singing a song in which all human beings join with him, rejoices in the presence of truth as our visible friend and hourly companion.

I find the whole of this section of the preface very difficult, but I believe Wordsworth to be expressing the notion of sharing. Though the poet says things the reader could never say, part of the point of his saying those things is that the reader can share them. And part of the reader's benefit is that he is privileged to share something with a superior person whose utterance is quite beyond the power of the reader's mouth. And it is no small privilege.

The sensation of sharing will be most obvious when the author deals with the most centrally human themes. Hamlet's soliloquies, the end of *Paradise Lost,* or, according to some readings, the fourth book of *Gulliver's Travels.*

I should now naturally go on to set forth the second way in which personality can find valuable expression in literature. But, in setting forth the first, the relation between personality in art to personality in life has perforce been touched on; and I had better say now what I have to say on the matter. I can at the same time say more about something I called a 'mental pattern', an entity about which Mr Lewis is very sceptical and which I described all too vaguely. I contrasted a man's practical or everyday personality with his more general and important 'mental pattern'; and in so doing appeared to belittle the former. Mr Lewis truly pointed out that in personality it is precisely the little things that count for so much. 'Where personality is in question I will not give up a wrinkle or a stammer.' And for Mr Lewis the very word *personality* suggests 'warmth and humanity, intimacy, the real rough and tumble of human life'.

I entirely concur with Mr Lewis's sentiments about wrinkles and stammers, and I think that his suspicion that I do not concur rests partly on my own vagueness of wording but partly on a confusion of two classes of things that should be separated. Our dispute began as follows. Mr Lewis speaking of a passage in *Hyperion* said it was not relevant that Keats should have first read about senators 'in a little brown book in a room smelling of boiled beef, the same day that he pulled out a loose tooth'. I agreed that these matters were accidents and I suggested that a man had a personality apart from them. Mr Lewis retorts that it is precisely these accidents that largely constitute the value to us of a personality in real life. And he instances wrinkles and stammers; but in so doing he is introducing into the discussion a new element, about which I had in no wise committed myself. Let me explain, taking the stammer as a convenient starting-point. Writing on a literary topic I cannot help thinking of the author with the most memorable stammer, Charles Lamb. Well, take Lamb's stammer as one kind of personal accident. But take the following imaginary happening, to which the word *accident* could be very properly applied. Lamb was once witnessing *Othello* with his favorite Bensley acting Iago. It is the middle of the third scene of the third act; and Lamb is keyed up to listen. Othello re-enters, and as Iago begins saying: 'Nor poppy, nor mandragora . . .', Lamb realises that his nose has begun violently to bleed. Holding his handkerchief to it he tries to get out. In his hurry he trips over the feet of a lady; he stumbles, he drops his handkerchief on her white dress with the worst possible results. Indignation in the neighbourhood at the commotion. He escapes humiliated. No well-constituted human being could consider such an accident as equivalent to Lamb's stammer. It is not a part of the person and it is something which decent feelings prompt us to ignore; anyhow quite trivial. Contrasted to this accident, Lamb's stammer is very important indeed, simply not to be put in the same class with it. Now Keats's hypothetical tooth, the brown book, and the smell of beef, are all trivialities, unrelated to anything essential in him. In fact it is doubtful if they should be included in 'personality' at all. This was the class of thing I meant by 'practical or everyday personality'. That I should have dismissed them from essential personality was no proof that I dismissed Lamb's stammer likewise.

What then is the nature of the wrinkles and stammers? They are valuable (and of course Mr. Lewis and I must agree here) because in spite of apparent triviality they express so much. They are indeed the minuter streaks of the human tulip we most of us delight to number, on the theory that the general is best expressed through the particular. They are to the man's life what the characteristic minutiae of his style are to his art. Far from rejecting or belittling them, I welcome them not only in themselves but as confirming my analogy between the personality expressed in life and that expressed in art.

I have reached the position of dismissing from any personal significance certain minutiae and of retaining others. It now remains for me to explain, if I can, how a 'mental pattern' is related to these significant minutiae. So far I have been speaking of personality in life, not in art, except when I made the smaller habits of style a parallel in art to the wrinkles and stammers in life. In speaking now of a 'mental pattern' I refer to something equally valid in both spheres, something allowing of expression in both life and art. I can describe it best through an analogy.

Conrad's *Typhoon* is the story of a middle-aged sea captain, who, till the time of the story, had never had his character fully tried. The trial comes in a typhoon, and he is equal to it. We are led to believe that the qualities that saved Conrad's captain had existed in some sort before the actual trial; it was no sudden and alien inspiration that helped him through. We know their existence only because of the trial, yet we know that they had been there all along in spite of our necessary ignorance should the trial never have taken place. In the same way a mental pattern consists of certain predispositions susceptible of many decrees of fulfillment or expression.

Of course these predispositions, as I call them, could not have been established without some acts of expression, acts which were not only expression but a creative agency. But any new act of expression is largely governed by the existing predispositions. It is this simple fact which makes Mr Lewis's dilemma, posed in his first essay, innocuous. Speaking of the passage in *Hyperion*, already much discussed, where Keats compares oaks to senators, Mr Lewis writes:

> The dilemma is as follows: are senators normally present to Keats whenever he sees, or thinks of, oaks? If they are not, then his normal consciousness of oaks is other than that which we come to enjoy in reading his poem.

And again about another passage in the same poem:

> Keats had to grope for his
> *gradual solitary gust*
> *Which comes upon the silence, and dies off,*
> *As if the ebbing air had but one wave.*
> But to grope for the words was to grope for the
> perception, for the one lives only in the other.

To these statements I reply: When Keats thought of his senators and his solitary gust, he certainly made something new, going beyond his old self. But it is equally true that there was something established in his mind ready to welcome the senators when they presented themselves to him. Present senators to a million other people, and they will not associate them with oaks; just because their cast of mind is not adjusted to make the creative effort to associate them. Keats made the association because among other reasons he was partly prepared to make it. It is the sum of Keats's preparednesses that constituted his mental pattern when he wrote *Hyperion*, part of which pattern he actually expressed in writing the poem. Of course in addition he altered those preparednesses by the very act of writing, and emerged a somewhat different person. Mr Lewis insists so strongly on the novelty of the perception in art and sets so little store by the accumulated predispositions that I am tempted to ask him whether in the sphere of life the man with the expressive wrinkle manufactures it afresh every time we notice it, having quite smoothed it away in the intervals. A question which brings up our problem: what is the relation of the wrinkles and stammers to the mental pattern? And here at once a distinction must be made. Speaking of stammers, do we mean an accident or a permanent characteristic? If we mean a single stammer that befell a man not prone to stammering, it has no connexion with the mental pattern; if a permanent proneness to stammer, it may have a very definite connexion. There are many ways of stammering or of manipulating wrinkles. If a man has accepted his stammers and wrinkles and made the best use of them (as a wise man does), they will show a general correspondence to that man's set of predispositions. And if that man is a writer, though he will not write stammeringly or make wrinkles the subject of his writings—stammers and wrinkles will make no apparent entry into his works— yet his style of writing will correspond to the style in which both stammers and wrinkles are manipulated. And helping to condition all three—style, stammers, and wrinkles— there lies behind them the mental pattern.

To communicate that pattern to us is part of the author's work, and to enjoy it, part of the reader's privilege. The more distinguished the pattern, the higher the privilege will be.

The above statement anticipates my more detailed description of the second way in which personality can operate in literature. To that description I will now lead up by referring to Mr Lewis's admirable account, already mentioned, of the sins of confounding the sphere of life with that of letters. In particular, he judges, austerely and convincingly, those who find in the illicit companionship of authors a compensation for their own social defects. Repelled by the defensive armour of their neighbours, they do the dirty on the defenceless shades of the illustrious dead. A horrible picture, yet let us not be too hasty, but judge an act by its fruit. I came across not long ago an instance of how a not dissimilar act, which by all the rules ought to have been disastrous, actually turned out well. One of the lessons, apparently incontrovertible, we have learnt from recent Shakespeare criticism is that it is illegitimate to allow to a dramatic character a life outside its context. A character exists for the work of art to which it belongs; and to tear it from its setting and then to romance about it is an act of wanton violence its creator could only have resented. Mr Lewis's remarks on live characters and characters in literature show that he agrees. Nevertheless, from E. T.'s beautiful and restrained memoir of D. H.

Lawrence we learn that it was precisely in this heinous way that he and the friends of his early manhood developed what was plainly a passionately felt and mentally fructifying love of literature. Without at all wishing to defend the sentimental debauch held by the maladjusted at the expense of the heroes of literature, I would suggest that such a debauch may have analogies with something legitimate and valuable.

Mr Lewis, instancing 'the rich, barren woman who loves her lap-dog too much and her neighbour too little', makes out a good case for even the dog's being a better substitute for good living than a dead poet can be. 'You can do something for the Peke; and it can make some response to you. . . . Unless you hold beliefs which enable you to obey the colophons of the old books by praying for the authors' souls, there is nothing you can do for a dead poet: and certainly he will do nothing for you.' To retort that you can read the dead poet is a quibble, but I am not sure that he can do nothing for us. However vicious it may be to use a dead poet to caress yourself on, there may yet be included in most exercises of such vice at least a fraction of a more elevated and a more active feeling. The female failure who uses the idea of Shelley as a substitute husband may in the very act get an inkling of a man who died while in process of making something good out of a gifted but imperfect nature subjected to uncommon mundane difficulties. And from that inkling she may derive a little strength to make a better job of her own particular problems. In other words a poet's personality may, through its being communicated in his art, exercise the homely function of setting an example. And indeed I believe that such a communication does in actual fact bring comfort and courage to people through this homely means. A recent critic of Milton, for instance, wrote of '"the debt of endless gratitude" that from my youth up I owe to Milton, whose property is to fortify the mind against "paralysing terrors" and false admirations; who is himself a far more romantic figure than Napoleon'. Perhaps Mr Lewis deprecates any reader's romancing thus about Milton; yet, if the impression of Milton's personality did in fact fortify the mind against paralysing terrors, is it not safer to forgo theory, however cogent apparently, and judge the tree by the fruit?

It is a simple fact that most of us to-day cannot in the course of ordinary life gain contact with people of the quality of the major poets, or, if we do, that contact is liable to be interrupted or spoiled in a hundred ways. We may look on a great poet as a supreme technician in words or a good watcher of other folk, yet he is in addition one whose

> *spirit's bark is driven,*
> *Far from the shore, far from the trembling throng*
> *Whose sails were never to the tempest given.*

And Milton spoke for all great poets when he said:

> No man apprehends what vice is as well as he who is truly virtuous; no man knows hell like him who converses most in heaven.

The great poet is one who has inhabited heavens and hells unbearable by the ordinary man, who has survived his residence, and who, in telling us of his experiences, can by his example help the ordinary man to make a better job of dealing with the smaller heavens and hells through which he must pass.

We complain of or rejoice in the elusiveness of Shakespeare's personality. Yet we are quite certain that he dared more than most men in his meditations on human fate, that he went so far as to imperil his mental equilibrium, but that having maintained it he reached a sanity richer than the normal. This personal triumph, so inspiring to weaker men, can be seen not in this or that character or in this or that play, but emerges from the whole series. Another example of personal daring expressed in poetry is

Baudelaire's. There is no need to approve or condemn the realms he explored; of his courage and control in exploring them there can be no doubt. With Achilles wondering at Priam's courage in coming to beg Hector's body we are impelled to say,

ἆ δείλ', ἦ δὴ πολλὰ κάκ' ἄνσχεο σὸν κατὰ θυμόν,
πῶς ἔτλης ἐπὶ νῆας Ἀχαιῶν ἐλθέμεν οἶος;

And though Baudelaire offers little inducement to others to follow his own particular line of exploration, his example may generate courage in other directions.

This talk of courage reminds me of some of Mr Lewis's analogies in his first essay. He puts the question of personality in terms of hunting or scouting. Admitting that the courage of the hunter or scout is important, he insists on keeping the quest separate from the courage that urges on the seeker.

> Even the reports of two scouts in war differ, and that with a difference traceable to personality: for the brave man goes farther and sees more; but the *value* of his report by no means consists in the fact that the intelligence officer, while he receives it, has the pleasure of meeting a brave man.

We agree in taking account of the courage; but I disagree over the whole analogy. Poetry is more complex than scouting, and what the poet brings back to us is both his report and the assurance of his own courage: the two sometimes inextricably interlocked.

Nor is it only the great adventurers among the poets who help us, through expressing their personalities. In life we sometimes meet people, not necessarily possessing any special gifts, who have made a quite exceptionally good job of their opportunities. In spite of shortcomings, difficulties, privations, or what not, they have made what we call a success of life. They have used all the material to hand and have arranged it in such a way as to give it the greatest possible significance. Once again the example of such people is very strong; to have known one of them may be a permanent influence on a man's life. Now some of the poets affect us in that way through their poetry. Andrew Marvell, for instance; writing on whom Mr Eliot ended his essay with the words, *c'était une belle âme, comme on ne fait plus à Londres,* and that after protesting the impersonality of Marvell's wit. Herrick, whom we have already discussed in a different context, is another. There is nothing very personal about a great many of Herrick's poems, yet one of the chief values of his poetry in bulk is the personality it reveals. Herrick did not have a particularly easy life. We are far too ready to assume that he was by instinct the adoring child of the English country-side and to mitigate the brutal rusticity of seventeenth-century Devon with unconscious memories of the comforts of Victorian Torquay. To break himself in to remote Devon after enjoying the best literary society in London was a tough job. But he succeeded in it; and it is this personal triumph, this resolute acquiescence in picking and enjoying the restricted range of rosebuds within his reach without wasting his energies in lamenting those beyond it, that give a general significance to his poetry. One of the main meanings of these apparently fragile and idyllic creations is a personal triumph of self-adjustment.

This should suffice to show the second class of thing I mean by personality in literature. And I should be very glad to think that Mr Lewis agreed that something of the sort is expressible in poetry, though I mind very little if he objects to applying the terms *personal* and *personality* to it.

I want now to guard myself against the charge of exaggerating the above element. First, let me admit that there are poets in whom the example of personality counts for very little; and the one that at once occurs to me is Tennyson. Tennyson was neither supremely courageous in meditating on human fate nor supremely skilful in making full use of his own gifts and the accidents of his life. Yet in his greatest work, in *The Lady of Shalott, Tithonas,* and parts of *In Memoriam* and *Maud* for instance, he tells us things that excite us and which we have not heard before. But he appears, as a vehicle of poetry, unusually passive. Or we can say that he had a superb unconscious which insisted from time to time on getting through, thanks of course to the pains he took to acquire a technical skill capable of meeting the demands likely to be made on it. Unfortunately, he came to trust his unconscious too little and he tried to check it rather than to follow its frightening vagaries. The result is that Tennyson did not make a very good job of himself and we tend to shrink from his personality.

Personality, then, has at least these two functions in literature. (It is the author's personality I speak of; that of the characters in a play or novel I do not distinguish from other counters or symbols.) It can benefit the reader, first by submitting itself to a special kind of sharing, and second by presenting him with a variety of example. Though personality seems to me to be important in both its functions, the last thing I wish to do is to limit literature to the task of expressing personality, even when it is most successful in just this task.

I wrote at the beginning of this paper that I thought Mr Lewis and I were beginning to approximate our opinions. But I am afraid that in actual fact I have spent most of my time in differing. All the same it is quite possible that we differ more in phraseology than in substance; and I shall now suggest that the word *personality* has for us different connotations and that if allowance could be made for these we might end in substantial agreement. But it remains possible that our differences are more fundamental and that they go beyond the question of personality altogether. And I shall end by trying to describe and to face that possibility.

There is no doubt that for Mr Lewis the word *personality* is primarily associated with the variegated details of living, while for me it is something more vague and more generalized. The result is that I apply personality to a class of feelings for which Mr Lewis has another name. The mental pattern I have described is something more embryonic than the clear-cut, perfected details he naturally thinks of. Examining that pattern, that set of predispositions, he would probably find all sorts of general impulses which he would consider to belong to the species or to the nation rather than to the person. And I freely admit that to say where group-consciousness leaves off and the individual consciousness begins must be quite impossible.

But if in my notion of personality I include a larger share of group-consciousness than he does, that does not mean that we are in serious disagreement. We may have similar notions about literature, only describe them differently.

I am now curious to know whether Mr Lewis finds my opinions, as restated, any more acceptable and whether he thinks our main subject of dispute can be resolved into no more than a matter of terminology. I hope, naturally, we may find ourselves agreeing after all. But whether or not we intend to approximate, the argument, if it is to continue, ought now, I think, to take another turn. Mr Lewis has said much about what literature is not, little about what it is. If it does not express the author's personality, should he not tell us what it does express? He has indeed dropped a few hints. I await eagerly his expansion of them.

V

In his last essay Dr Tillyard is kind enough to express a hope that our controversy is gradually bringing us into agreement. In certain respects I think it is; and even where agreement may not be possible, the grounds of disagreement are being made clearer. To this second process Dr Tillyard makes an important contribution when he reminds us, as theorists are too seldom reminded, how much our doctrines owe to real differences of imaginative experience rooted in our 'mental tempers' (or perhaps even in our physiology) which can be unmasked only by 'frank personal testimony'.[1] At the outset I wish to put on record my personal testimony to a character in my experience which may possibly differentiate it from Dr Tillyard's. On pp. 91 and 92 above Dr Tillyard invites us to distinguish three possible senses of the word *unique*. The first means 'improbability of recurrence'; the second an experience 'allying us however distantly to the poet and the mystic'. The third, illustrated by a delightful quotation from Jane

---
[1] p. 94.

Austen, means a quality found only in works of art and in people. Now it is a mere matter of fact that I find no such distinction in my own experience. I trust no one will call me a mystic—a name, in its strict theological sense, too high, and in its popular use (I hope) too vague, to describe me; but it appears to me that all sorts of objects, animate and inanimate, natural and artificial, give me just that kind of experience which Dr Tillyard describes under his third species of uniqueness. The rains and sunsets that I spoke of seem to me unique not only by being irrecoverable; they seem, like Jane Austen's niece, 'so odd and all the time so perfectly natural'. They respond, like chords of music, to some want within, unnoticed till the moment of its fulfillment. They fit the senses and imagination like an old glove. Momentary as they are, they seem (I hardly know how to say it) to have been prepared from all eternity for their precise place in the symphony of things—to be parts of a score rather than cross-sections of a process. Nor does 'kinship' and 'sharing' lack, in the only sense in which I find them in works of art. Does not 'our heart fly into the breast of the bird'? Do we not almost feel the strain of fibres as a tree bends to the wind? I have passed from statements to questions because, as usual, when we actually face it, any fundamental difference between our own experience and that of a fellow man refuses to be believed. There must be some mistake: one or both of us must be saying what he does not mean; and I for my part submit that a false exaltation of poetry has led Dr Tillyard to overlook that downright *interestingness* in the real world which meets, or even besieges, him daily whenever he is not ill, or tired, or preoccupied. One of my chief grievances against the Personal Heresy and its inevitable attendant Poetolatry, is that disparagement of common things and common men which they induce. If we can open our eyes on poetry only by closing them on the universe, then 'would we had never seene Wertenberge, never read booke!'

For this reason I am troubled when Dr Tillyard speaks of the awful or enchanting realities mentioned by the poets as 'counters or symbols'. 'Symbols' I do not object to; but the suggestion is that all symbols are of the same order as counters—that a beautiful woman (or for that matter a glow-worm) has no value in herself, receives all her significance from the poets, as little disks of coloured bone receive their value from the arbitrary agreement of the gamblers. Two kinds of symbol must surely be distinguished. The algebraical symbol comes naked into the world of mathematics and is clothed with value by its masters. A poetic symbol—like the Rose, for Love, in Guillaume de Lorris—comes trailing clouds of glory from the real world, clouds whose shape and colour largely determine and explain its poetic use. In an equation, *x* and *y* will do as well as *a* and *b*; but the *Romance of the Rose* could not, without loss, be re-written as the *Romance of the Onion*, and if a man did not see why, we could only send him back to the real world to study roses, onions, and love, all of them still untouched by poetry, still raw. Of these distinctions I do not for one moment suppose that Dr Tillyard is ignorant; but I think his language encourages us to neglect them.

These preliminaries are important for the theory of poetry which I am presently going to propound in answer to the challenge delivered at the end of Dr Tillyard's essay; but before proceeding to that theory I must deal with a few minor disagreements and agreements. Dr Tillyard has given the poet's personality two functions: 'it can benefit the reader by a special kind of sharing and by presenting him with a variety of examples'. About the exemplary function—illustrated by Dr Tillyard in his humorous, yet charitable, picture of the 'female failure' and her Shelley—I do not think we need differ. A poet is, of course, a man, and any man may be used as an example by those who admire him. And I will even admit that a poet may be more exemplary, *ceteris paribus*, than another man; for though I do not think that poetry consists in self-expression, I am far from denying that much may be learnt of the poet's self from his works and that his example may therefore reach many generations. What I cannot allow is that the poet exercises this function *quâ* poet; or that to follow his example is to use his poetry, *quâ* poetry. And this, I contend, is not a straw-splitting distinction. It is clear that many artefacts can be used for purposes for which they were not intended; and it is also clear that the examination of such accidental uses tells us nothing about the specific functions. You can make a poultice out of porridge or use a thin volume of Shakespeare's sonnets to support a rickety table, but these facts seem to me quite irrelevant to the theory of cookery or the theory of poetry. You can use a poet, not as a poet, but as a saint or hero; and if your poet happens to have been a saintly or heroic man as well as a poet you may even be acting wisely. If there lives any man so destitute of all traditions human and divine and so unfortunate in his acquaintance that he can find no better example among the living or the dead than Shelley or Baudelaire, I no more blame him for following them than we blame a castaway on an island for making shift to use a pen-knife as a saw. But my pity will not induce me to say that pen-knives are made for sawing. That the poet, treated as saint or hero, is similarly used for an alien purpose, may easily be seen by asking whether our submission to his example varies in proportion to our poetical appreciation;

and I am sure it does not. If it did, I should think *Irene* a greater tragedy than *Tamburlaine* and Lamb a better poet than Coleridge. A young woman, or a young man either, may use Shelley as Dr Tillyard suggests; they may use him also for learning the English language or Greek mythology, or even spelling. But all these uses surely fall outside the theory of poetry.

On the question of 'sharing' there is almost complete agreement between us. When I first threw the apple of discord in 1933 I already welcomed the view that 'we approach the poet by *sharing* his consciousness, not by studying it', that we 'look with his eyes, not at him'.[2] Whatever difference still separates us here is one of emphasis. I am still anxious, as I was anxious in 1933, to stress the distinction between two relations which tend to be confused—that of sharing, co-operation or companionship on the one hand, and that of reciprocity on the other. We speak of lovers as being in sympathy, and so, of course, they usually are on a variety of topics. But if we take the word *sympathy* in its strict sense (a 'feeling together', a joint or shared experience) it must be remembered that mutual love is the very opposite of sympathy. The man is attending to the woman and ignoring himself, the woman is attending to

---

[2] p. 14.

the man and ignoring herself. So far from sharing a feeling, they are having *opposite* feelings; feelings as unlike and as mutually exclusive as their physical functions in the act of union. 'My true love has my heart and I have his': in proportion to the degree of love, the one mind is occupied with just that which the other excludes. Real sympathy, on the other hand—as of two boys sailing a boat or two men looking at a sunset—implies a common interest; the parties forget themselves not in each other but in a third thing. In this sense, paradoxically enough, it may even be said that two rivals who love the same woman are more in 'sympathy' than two lovers. No doubt, in human life the relations are constantly mixed. The lovers, in the ordinary course of nature, pass on from interest in each other to a common interest in their children: the two boys learn to like each other because they both like sailing boats. And so, as I have already admitted,[3] our imaginative sharing of the poet's eyes will sometimes throw up in its course an emotion directed towards the poet. There is no difference here between Dr Tillyard's view and mine, provided always that we both regard the reading of poetry as essentially a co-operation, sharing or sympathy between the poet and ourselves, which, like all truly sympathetic or

---

[3] p. 82.

co-operative experiences, is directed towards a third thing. We lose ourselves not in the poet but in that wherein he is lost—in the adventures of Crusoe, the flowing of the Oxus, or the rotundity of Falstaff.

But even when this has been freely admitted, I still feel myself obliged to ask, as I asked in my first essay, what precisely we are sharing, and whether it can be unambiguously described as the poet's personality. Marvell's poem *The Mower to the Glow-worms* will here serve very well, and the precise force of my question can be brought out by a dilemma. In the poem it is feigned that a lover goes about addressing some rather defeatist advice to a number of insects. Now this is either true or false in the plain historical sense. If it is true, if the man Marvell actually behaved as the lover is feigned to behave, then that man is a lunatic, his experience is shared, if at all, only by other lunatics, and is interesting only to alienists. If it is false, then the merit of the poem lies in the success with which these fictions communicate to us a mood which in itself involved no lunacy, no conversations with glow-worms, and perhaps—if we accept Dr Tillyard's suggestion that Julia has only the function of a corset—no love. But since we, the readers, find this mood congenial and accept it, it follows that the difference between Marvell and ourselves does not lie in the capacity for such moods; or, in other words, that what we share is not Marvell's idiosyncrasy but that part of Marvell which is common to us and him; perhaps to all men. What differentiates us from Marvell is something we do not necessarily share in reading the poem—the skill, namely, and invention which enable him to communicate. But personality must surely be a *principium individuationis,* that which distinguishes one man from another. It would seem, therefore, that the reading of poetry usually involves not a sharing of the poet's personal or idiosyncratic experience but of his merely human experience. What is peculiar to the poet is not the thing he communicates, nor even the symbols whereby he communicates, but his power of finding and using them—in fact, as we might have anticipated, the art of poetry.

This, I have said, is the 'usual' situation. I have been forced to qualify my doctrine in this way, because I believe there are two kinds of poetry. The commonest, and by wide human agreement the greatest, kind operates as I have described; it communicates such experiences as all men have had, so that simple readers exclaim 'How true', and classicists call it a 'just representation of general nature', and realists say that the poet is stripping off the mask of convention and facing 'the facts'. But I must admit that there are also poems which seem to give me a new and nameless sensation, or even a new sense, to enrich me with experience which nothing in my previous life had prepared me for. When this happens, I do not deny that we are sharing something peculiar to the poet. But if this is a condition present in some poems and absent from others, it cannot be brought into our definition of poetry. Still less can we say that it is a necessary character of the greatest poetry. Complexionally, I like this second kind very much: to the natural man in me it is at times more congenial than any other. But the weight of critical opinion forbids me to call it the better of the two. I do not find it in Homer, Sophocles, Chaucer, Spenser, Milton, or (*pace* the Abbé Brémond) in Racine: I find it seldom in Virgil, and only in the very latest works of Shakespeare; but I find it abundantly in Blake, in the early Morris, in Mr De la Mare and Miss Sitwell, in Mr Eliot, and even in Poe. I find it most of all in the prose work of George Macdonald, where literary competence is often so to seek that any of us could improve even the best passages very materially in half an hour. Clearly such a quality must not be identified with poetry; and indeed it is so troublesome that I am glad to have it out of the argument on almost any terms. For my own part I am sure that I do not care for these things because they introduce me to the men Morris and Macdonald: I care for the books, and the men, because they witness to these things, and it is the message not the messenger that has my heart. But for our present purpose it is enough to have shown that such peculiarity is not essential to poetry. It is simply *one of the things* that poetry can be used for.

I have been challenged by Dr Tillyard to produce my own theory of poetry, and it is now time to begin doing so with the proposition (not, surely, very paradoxical) that poetry is an art or skill—a trained habit of using certain instruments to certain ends. This platitude is no longer unnecessary; it has been becoming obscured ever since the great romantic critics diverted our attention from the fruitful question, 'What kind of composition is a poem?' to the barren question, 'What kind of man is a poet?' The second question is barren, because the only true answer ('A poet is a man who makes poems') immediately throws us back on the first question which we ought to have asked at the outset. The romantic critics, however, were not content with the true answer. Wordsworth begins by saying that a poet 'is a man speaking to men', which unfortunately includes all men not mad or dumb: to confine it to poets we need an account of that special mode of speaking which poets use and others do not. Instead of supplying this he goes on to attribute to the poet a superiority over other men in a number of qualities such as 'tenderness', 'enthusiasm', and 'sensibility'. Such a theory of poetry I call Naturalistic, because it is concerned not with a human and voluntary activity called poetry, but with 'poethood' conceived as an intrinsic, natural superiority in certain favored individuals, like beauty or stature. This would be more tolerable if the superiority claimed were any of those really relevant to poetical composition. If it were said, 'A poet is a man who can invent stories or at least fill in other people's stories with plausible and interesting detail', or again, 'A poet is a man with a taste for words, a man more than ordinarily sensible to their associations, flavours and sounds', the theory would be less objectionable. We should only have to add to it the caution that these bents or talents, even if they be as natural in the first instance as the hand of the future surgeon or the ear of the future piano-tuner, can reach poethood only by training, industry, and the method of trial and error. But full-blown Naturalism defines the poet by qualities no more connected with literary composition than with many other activities. It wants poets to be a separate race of great souls or *mahatmas*. Poetolatry is its natural result, for if there were such a race of supermen among us, those who know no higher deity would do well to worship them.

The simplest answer to Naturalism is that it cannot, from the very nature of the case, be proved. When Dr Tillyard says that the poet 'has inhabited heavens and hells unbearable by the ordinary man', we may reply, 'How do you know?' The poet can tell: the ordinary man cannot. Even those who think that the poet expresses only himself, at least admit that expression is his job. But if so, what fair comparison can there be between the experiences of the professional expressor and those of the inarticulate many? It is like saying, 'All discovered islands have better harbours than all undiscovered islands.' I admit that some writers have told me for the first time of heavens and hells I never met before; but many, equally great or greater, have told me only of those we all have to bear whether we choose to call them 'unbearable' or not. What hells can be harder to bear than those in which many of our unpoetic fellow creatures live? What man, after forty years in the world, has not experience enough (if that were all that was needed) to be raw material for all the tragedies of Shakespeare? Once again, the view I am fighting depends on a gross under-estimation of common things and common men. 'To be a man', as Professor Tolkien recently reminded us, 'is tragedy enough.' Yes, and comedy enough too. The Naturalistic doctrine is a mere assumption, first made by the arrogance of poets and since accepted by the misdirected humility of an irreligious age. When once the instinct for reverence is 'To Let', plenty of tenants will offer themselves: with this 'all Europe rings from side to side'.

But our answer to Naturalism is more than a plea of 'Not proven'. The rude, but inevitable, retort to Wordsworth's definition is 'go and look at a few poets'. Courtesy to our contemporaries must not forbid us to point out that a poet, an admitted and unmistakable poet, is sometimes (in certain periods, often) a man inferior to the majority in 'tenderness', 'enthusiasm', and 'knowledge of human nature'—not to speak of information, common-sense, fortitude, and courtesy. The 'Dirty Twenties' of our own century produced poems which succeeded in communicating moods of boredom and nausea that have only an infinitesimal place in the life of a corrected and full-grown man. That they were poems, the fact of communication and the means by which it was effected, are, I take it, sufficient proof. But the experience communicated was certainly not that of spiritual supermen; if it truly reflected the personality of the poets, then the poets differed from the mass, if at all, only by defect. We do well to praise the art and show charity to the men. But they are not great souls. Wash their feet, and I will praise your humility: sit at their feet, and you will be a fool. Yet they made poems.

Finally, if there were no other ground for condemning Naturalism, the results it produces in criticism are ground enough. It leads Dr Tillyard to ask me whether a man with a stammer or a wrinkle produces it afresh every time I meet him, as I believe that a poet makes poetry afresh whenever he achieves a poem. The question shows how completely the distinctions between art and nature, act and event, deliberate and involuntary, have been obliterated. The wrinkle remains because it is nature, something that happens to a man; the poetry does not, because it is something a man has to do. Thus again, Naturalism leads Dr Tillyard into something very like ranking poets according to their 'Courage' in 'meditating on human fate'. Indeed, indeed, a soldier ought not to have written thus. I know that we hear much of this kind of courage in publishers' advertisements: there every scribbler is 'daring' when he defies gods whom he does not believe in, or conventions that have no authority in the only circles he frequents. But had not 'courage' of this sort better be left to blurb-writers? For, to tell the truth, literary composition is not an employment that makes very heavy demands on this arduous virtue. What meditation on human fate demands so much 'courage' as the act of stepping into a cold bath? I should be glad to hear of it, for I know no path to heroism which sounds so suited to my own capacities.

Rejecting Naturalism, then, I turn to the small number of tentative opinions which constitute my own theory of poetry; and by poetry I mean, as the renaissance critics meant, imaginative literature whether in prose or verse. In the first place, I believe poetry to be an art or skill. A skill is usually defined by its instruments. I suppose we shall all agree that the instrument of poetry is language. But since language is used for other purposes, such as philosophy and commerce, we now need the *differentia* of the poetical use of language. Taking conversation as the common base, I would say that scientific or philosophical language, on the one hand, and poetical language on the other, are alternative improvements of this in the direction of two different kinds of efficiency. Thus if we take the sentence 'This is cold' we can make it more precise either by saying, 'This is twice as cold as that', or by saying, 'Ugh! It's like a smack in the face'. The first proceeds by turning a qualitative sensation into a quantity; the second, by communicating with the aid of an emotive noise and a simile just that quality which the other neglects. Following the first process further you will come to science, which escapes from the sensuous altogether into that world of pure quantities which is so much more useful for what Bacon called 'operation'. Following the second far enough, you will come to poetry, that is, to a skill or trained habit of using all the extra-logical elements of language—rhythm, vowel-music, onomatopoeia, associations, and what not—to convey the concrete reality of experiences. The ideal limit of the one process is actually reached in pure arithmetic; whether the ideal of the other has been reached—whether 'pure poetry' exists or not—need not now be discussed. The vast majority of human utterances fall between the two extremes. It is therefore not usually possible, and it is never necessary, to say of a composition in any absolute sense, 'This is poetry': what we can say is, 'This is further in the poetical direction than that'. But as, in ordinary terminology, we mean by a tall man or a rich man one who is taller or richer than most, so by a poem we mean a composition which communicates more of the concrete and qualitative than our usual utterances do. A poet is a man who produces such compositions more often and more successfully than the rest of us.

In a stricter terminology, however, nearly all men are poets, in the sense that they can and do exploit the extra-logical properties of language to produce utterances of the concrete which have a value higher than zero. We do not usually call them poets: just as I am not called a carpenter though I could, at a pinch, put up some sort of a shelf, nor a doctor, though I know the use of a few common drugs. Even when such compositions use verse and are committed to writing and have a value quite sensibly higher than zero, we do not usually call their authors poets, reserving that name, as utility bids us, for those who do the thing specially well. Thus a man might be a 'poet' by the standards of one society and not by those of another—as a man might be 'tall' among the Japanese, and 'short' among the Norwegians.

The difference between scientific or philosophical language and poetical language is emphatically not that the first utters truths and the second fancies. On the contrary everything that is concrete is real,[4] and some suspect that everything real is concrete. The abstractions used by science and philosophy may or may not be the names of universals which are timeless realities as Plato thought; but they are not the names of 'real things' in the popular sense—things that occur in space and time. In space and time there is no such thing as an organism, there are only animals and vegetables. There are no mere vegetables, only trees, flowers, turnips, &c. There are no 'trees', except beeches, elms, oaks, and the rest. There is even no such thing as 'an elm'. There is only *this* elm, in such a year of its age at such an hour of the day, thus lighted, thus moving, thus acted on by all the past and all the present, and affording such and such experiences to me and my dog and the insect on its trunk and the man a thousand

---

[4] i.e., is a real something, though not necessarily the thing it pretends to be: e.g., what pretends to be a crocodile may *be* a (real) dream; what pretends at the breakfast-table to be a dream may *be* a (real) lie.

miles away who is remembering it. A real elm, in fact, can be uttered only by a poem. The sort of things we meet in poetry are the only sort we meet in life—things unique, individual, lovely, or hateful. Unfortunately, however, poetry does not, as poetry, tell us whether the particular ones she describes do, in fact, exist. That is where science comes in. In order to assert facts, i.e., to predict experiences, she must infer: in order to infer she must abstract. Only science can tell you where and when you are likely to meet an elm: only poetry can tell you what meeting an elm is like. The one answers the question *Whether*, the other answers the question *What*. We abstract to inquire whether God exists: Dante shows you what it would be like if He did, or, in other words, gives a meaning to the mere abstraction 'existence of God', and though he cannot, as a poet, foretell the conclusion of your debate, tells you what it is you are really debating about. Abstraction is very like money. Neither gold nor paper is real wealth, but it is more convenient than real wealth for purposes of exchange. Poetry has the real wealth which the abstractions represent, but this is too cumbersome for the commerce of thought.

Each of these two kinds of language is admirable for what it does, not for what it fails to do. It is no advantage to philosophic language that it fails to reach the concrete, and no advantage to poetry that it cannot prove the existence of anything—any more than a man's inability to suckle children is an advantage, or a woman's inability to bowl overarm. The fact that we cannot be philosophic and poetic in any high degree at the same moment is, I take it, an unmitigated evil. If there exist anywhere in the universe creatures as far above us as we are above the dogs, presumably their language combines at every moment the clarity and cogency of Euclid with the warmth and solidity of Shakespeare. They can always in the same breath demonstrate *that* a thing is and present to you *what* it is. Again, though it is convenient to define things *per differentiam*, it is a logical blunder to suppose that the point of maximum differentiation between them always coincides with the greatest value. Of course, in a given treatise a poetical element of the wrong sort may spoil the argument, and an argument may spoil a given poem; but it is not true in general that the two kinds of composition are best when they are most unlike. The worst philosophers are often the most jejune, and the worst poets the most unreasonable. Locke and Poe are further apart than Plato and Dante.

Hitherto we have succeeded only in defining poetic language; but language must be about something. You cannot just 'say', you must say this or that. It is time, therefore, to set down what little I can about the content of poetry. It will be convenient to remind ourselves that we took conversation as the common base on which all improved uses of language were raised. Returning to this, we can now proceed by elimination. Whatever in ordinary conversation is concerned with proving anything is clearly embryonic science or philosophy, and will not be part of the content of poetry. Again, whatever in a conversation has a practical purpose conditioned by the proximity of the speakers in space and time ('Hand me the salt'—'Don't be angry') will not find a place in that written and lasting poetry to which we usually give the name; though dramatic or fictional imitations of such speech may well occur in it. But when these obvious eliminations have been made, I fear that we can make no more. These two forms of conversation excepted, the truth seems to be that the number of things you can write poetry about is the same as the number of things you can talk about. Being a skill of utterance, it can be used to utter almost anything; to draw attention to (though not, of course, to demonstrate) a fact, to tell lies, to tell admitted fictions, to describe your own real or feigned emotions, to make jokes.

For this reason many discussions about 'Literature'—as if literature were a single homogeneous thing like water—are discussions about a nonentity. Poetry is not a low nor a lofty, a useful or a mischievous, a grave or a trivial, a 'true' or a 'false' activity, any more than 'saying' is. In that sense there is really no such thing as literature—only a crowd of people using concrete language as well as they can to talk about anything that happens to interest them. It differs sharply in this respect from an art like Music. You can, if you like, both make and hear a sonata without thinking of anything but sounds. But you cannot write or read one word of a poem by thinking only about poetry. The first note of the sonata has no necessary reference to anything beyond music; the first word of *Paradise Lost* (*of*) is from the very beginning the sign of a relation which exists outside that poem and outside poetry altogether. This is the necessary condition of an art of 'saying': you must say something.

It follows that, in a certain sense, poetry is not an 'Art' at all. It is by art or skill that the poets contrive to utter concretely what they want to say; but the thing said is not 'Art'—it is something more like a remark. The skill which went to the utterance of it has all the privileges of art; it is exempt (like plumbing or boot-blacking) from moral and logical criticism, and it is best judged by fellow artists. To claim similar immunities for the thing said is a confusion. I will let the plumber tell me how culpable his predecessor was in allowing my scullery to get flooded; I will not let him decide *whether* it is flooded, still less whether it ought to be.

On the other hand, while it is thus useful to remember that poetry is an art of 'saying' we must beware of a misunderstanding. What the poet 'says' must not be identified with the apparent (i.e., the grammatical) propositions in his poem. This is the error which Dr I. A. Richards has so long and usefully combated—the error under which the late Professor Babbitt, though wise, wrote much of his *Rousseau and Romanticism*. The poet is not 'saying' that his soul is an enchanted boat. Poetry is an exploitation of language to convey the concrete; one of the means by which it does this is a free use of propositions which have logically only the remotest connexion with its real utterance. What it 'says' is the total, concrete experience it gives to the right reader—the πεπαιδευμένος. The means are art; the thing conveyed, said, or uttered is not. It is everybody's business.

It follows that there is an ambiguity in the expression 'a great poet'. The skill of concrete utterance, as we have seen, can be used for almost any purpose. Fools use it to utter folly, wise men to utter wisdom, humorous men to make jokes, and vermin to utter poison. It can be used (like the telephone) by great men and little—by any one who can acquire the skill. This skill is, of course, a very difficult one but it can be acquired by men whose *general* level of capacity is low. The same is true of other highly difficult skills—a great surgeon, a great chess player, a great calculator, a great financier, may be by no means a great man. By a 'great poet' we may therefore mean one of two things. We may mean a great man—a man excelling others in knowledge, wisdom, and virtue—who is also a poet and who uses his poetical skill for the utterance of great things. On the other hand we may mean merely a man who is greatly a poet, who possesses this skill in a high or 'great' degree—as we speak of a great cricketer, a great walker, or even a great bore. A great bore need not be a great man, he need only be greatly boring. A man may show himself greatly poetical by using all the resources of the art of utterance to communicate something that is of no general interest at all. I say of 'general' interest because many worthless experiences may be as *difficult* to convey in their concrete entirety as valuable ones, and their conveyance may therefore be of technical interest to other artists.

The reverence for 'great poets'—*pii vates et Phoebo digna locuti*—is natural in periods when the art of poetry attracts great men. Every art, however, has its ups and downs. The schoolmaster was a slave in Rome and a potentate in Victorian England; the prostitute, an abject in the eighteenth century, was sometimes honoured in ancient Greece; the actor's profession in the last years of Paganism reached depths from which it took centuries to recover. Similarly there are periods when poetry falls into inferior hands. Its practitioners, using their skill for trivial, perverse, or merely imbecile purposes, may nevertheless possess that skill in a high degree—may be 'greatly poetical'. There is then a danger that they will claim and enjoy that reverence and authority which are due only to great men using poetry.

It will naturally be asked, what, in my view, the true value of poetry is, and who the right judges are. Indeed, my admission that 'great poetry' means, in one of its senses, poetry by great men, may seem to lead us back to the personal heresy. But we have already explained that poetry does not take over from ordinary conversation any of those utterances whose value depends on the proximity of the speakers in space and time. It shares with conversation those utterances, and those only, whose value can survive detachment from their original social context: not the love-making and quarrelling, not the 'contacts', the friendships, and the affections, but on the contrary the stories, the jokes, the reflections. It preserves not primarily what excites love, but what contributes to amusement, entertainment, wisdom, or edification; in fact those parts of conversation which are worth *repeating*.

It follows that the best judge of poetry is he who can best judge of human utterances, who can best say what is dull or interesting, what is stale or fresh, what edifies or corrupts, what gives delight or disgust. Of this ideal judge we can give no definition. He is simply Aristotle's πεπαιδευμένος. This lame conclusion will, I fear, provoke a storm of derision, but we must not allow ourselves to be moved by it. For behind this derision lurks an absolutely fatal demand; the demand that there should be professional experts to classify poetry as there are professional chemists to classify chemicals. It is an attempt to strip the creature Man of one more prerogative, to hand something more over to his permanent civil servants. Whether we regard it as fortunate or unfortunate, the fact is that there is no *essential* qualification for criticism more definite than general wisdom and health of mind. To make such wisdom effective, many conditions may be necessary, such as a really good knowledge of the language and a wide experience of poetry.

It is in virtue of the latter that poets—who are usually readers of poetry—may sometimes have a better chance, *ceteris paribus*, of being good critics than other men have. But they are exposed to their own dangers. The professional will 'smell of the shop'; he will have the lop-sided sensibility of the expert and the expert's tendency to consider the value of the thing done too little and the difficulty of the doing too much. It would, moreover, be a false delicacy to overlook the common interests, and also the disinterested *cameraderie*, which inevitably attach him to his own profession. This must specially be taken into account in an age when the old balance of power between poets, booksellers, critics, and readers has been overthrown—when 90 per cent of the readers are themselves poets, anxious candidates for admission to the dominant group, when poets are also anonymous reviewers, and perhaps editors and publishers. I do not mean to insult any one; I am not suggesting that poets are less scrupulous than any other profession, but only (in the light of much historical evidence) that they are not more scrupulous. Encouraged by poetolatry from without, and from within by the universal modern tendency to trusts and combines, to increasing efficiency, solidarity, and secrecy of organization, they would be men of heroic virtue if they remained perfectly unbiased critics. It is here that the much-abused academic critic can supply a corrective. He may have his own prejudices, but he is exempt from some temptations.

Where the πεπαιδευμένος is to be found may be indicated by the contrasted stories of Mr A and Mr B. Mr A had never read a line of poetry till he came to Oxford. There he suddenly found himself, on the strength of a few introductions, in a literary set. A world of first editions, 'movements', periodicals, and gossip about great contemporaries, burst on him with the suddenness of a tropic dawn. He became a reader of poetry in three weeks and a poet in six. He met one of the great. He saw himself in print. He is now a free-lance journalist, living in the heart of the movement, keeping well up to date, reading every one, meeting every one, reviewing every one, being reviewed by every one; and he knows, if possible, even more about the future of literature than about its present. Mr B, on the other hand, has never, I am afraid, read anything beyond the first page except because he liked it. He developed this habit at about the age of ten, and he had discovered most of the English poets, on wet days, before he was fifteen. He lived in an unliterary family and never dreamed that his taste for poetry was a ground for commendation. He has learned to like some of the moderns, but he reads only the ones he likes. I never could drive into his head the concept of 'importance' in poetry. He always wants to know if it is good, and whether I think he would enjoy it. He can't read many reviews; indeed—if it is not incredible—he once found a favourable review of a book of his own too dull to finish. He is very ill informed. If I wanted to find out what is going on I should certainly ask Mr A. But in sheer criticism, Mr B is the man for my money.

So much for the judges; what of the value? The truth is that the value of literature, as of other utterances, has always been pretty well understood by the great mass of readers. Of any utterance, whether conversational or poetical, our first demand is that it should be interesting. I am afraid we cannot make it more definite than that. It may be interesting for all sorts of reasons; because it is so funny, because it is so true, because it is so unexpected, or because it does just what we were expecting so well, because it carries us away from daily life into such fine regions of fantasy, or because it brings us back to our immediate surroundings with such a home-felt sense of reality. I know that different things interest different people. It cannot be helped. That is interesting *simpliciter* which interests the wise man. And in the second place, we demand that an utterance, besides entertaining, charming, or exciting us for the moment should have a desirable permanent effect on us if possible—should make us either happier, or wiser, or better. There is nothing 'moral' in the narrower sense about this, though morals come into it. It is all of a piece with what we want in other departments of life: a man wants his food to be nourishing as well as palatable, his games to be healthy as well as enjoyable, his wife to be a good companion and housekeeper as well as a pleasing sexual mate. I conclude, then, that the old critics were perfectly right when they demanded of literature the *utile* and the *dolce, solas* and *doctryne*, pleasure and profit. All attempts to produce a neater or more impressive scheme have, in my opinion, failed. The only two questions to ask about a poem, in the long run, are, firstly, whether it is interesting, enjoyable, attractive, and secondly, whether this enjoyment wears well and helps or hinders you towards all the other things you would like to enjoy, or do, or be.

The value of a poem consisting in what it does to the readers, all questions about the poet's own attitude to his utterance are irrelevant. The question of his 'sincerity' or 'disinterestedness' should be forever banished from criticism. The dyslogistic terms *insincere, spurious, bogus, sham*, &c., are mere emotive noises, signifying that the speaker is unwilling to keep silence, but has not yet discovered what is wrong with the poem. Unable to answer the real question, 'What, in this series of words, excites a feeling of hostility which prevents enjoyment?' he invents answers to the irrelevant question, 'What was the poet's state of mind when he wrote?'

The most characteristic contents of literary utterances are stories—accounts of events that did not take place. The primary value of these is that they are interesting. But why they interest, and in what different ways, and what permanent results they produce in the reader, I do not profess to know. Oddly enough, criticism has discussed this very little. Between Aristotle and the modern mythographical school of Miss Maud Bodkin, Professor Wilson Knight, and Professor D. G. James, we find almost nothing. It is in this direction, I suggest, that critical effort can be most profitably expended.

It will be seen that the tendency of my theory is, in some degree, to lower the status of the poet as poet. But that is because I think the only hope for poetry now lies in lowering his status. Unless he speedily returns to the workmanlike humility of his great predecessors and submits to the necessity of interesting and pleasing as a preliminary to doing anything else, the art of poetry will disappear from among us altogether. It may be that in the past we took too little pains to hear the difficult tune that some new poets were playing; but we have now learnt our lesson too well. *The Ugly Duckling* has stuck too deep in our minds, and we are afraid to condemn any abortion lest it should prove in the end to be a swan. It is high time to remember another story in Hans Andersen which teaches a lesson at least equally important. It is called *The Emperor's New Clothes*.

VI

I had hoped, after writing my second contribution, that my third might be relatively free from controversial argument and consist mainly of statement. But on reading Mr Lewis's last instalment I see that controversy cannot be avoided. Although I am sorry to be contradictious when my opponent has agreed to say no more, I am glad to find refuge in controversy from the obligation of conducting a prolonged soliloquy on the question of what poetry is about. A soliloquy; for though Mr Lewis has said at length what poetry *is*, he is brief on the question of what poetry is about.[1] That baby, after a very cursory fondling, he has handed me to make the best of. He commits himself to saying that poetry is characteristically concerned with interesting stories and can be concerned with almost anything, but he refrains from detailed treatment. In fact, I have failed to draw him on this topic; and perhaps he has been wise, for it is very forbidding. And I am not sorry if,

---

[1] Because, in my view, this is like the question, 'What do people talk about?' Infinity must be represented by brief symbols. C.S.L.

before having to face it, I cannot avoid joining issue with him on several others.

First, I retain my distinction between the kinds of sharing we experience when we have to do with inanimate nature and animals on the one hand and with authors on the other. When we 'almost feel the strain of fibres as a tree bends to the wind', it is a case not of sympathy but of empathy; it is the 'old, old tale of Narcissus'. We are not playing a game with another player, but, like a child, with ourselves. Often, too, the experience contains elements that are the very opposite of sharing. We rejoice because the world we view is so separate from us, because we feel how little its business has to do with us, how admirably it can get on without us. This is the ruling factor in a discriminating delight in cats. I fancy, too (against the views of more learned critics of Hopkins), that when the poet's 'heart in hiding stirred for a bird', he does at that moment see the windhover in precisely this detached manner. He is in hiding, and the bird's utter unconsciousness of his admiring gaze is a part of the experience. But unlike bending trees, cats, and kestrels, poems invite us to share their authors' feelings. And, if we comply, we get something that trees, cats, and kestrels cannot give. Of course this is not to decry trees, cats, and kestrels, or to imply that the two different experiences are mutually exclusive.

Mr Lewis (p. 120) agrees that poets may be examples, but pleads that this is not the thing by which they are poets. 'You can use a poet, not as a poet, but as a saint or hero', but, he argues, that is not his true function. Here, I agree as regards poets, yet I would quote Mr Lewis's words from a later page (p. 136) to the effect that 'though it is convenient to define things *per differentiam*, it is a logical blunder to suppose that the point of maximum differentiation between them always coincides with the greatest value'. Precisely; the poet is not a poet because he sets an example, but the setting of an example may be of more value than the thing which makes him a poet and not something else. In passing I must protest against the implication that saints are saints and heroes heroes through their exemplary function. On the contrary, saints are saints because they achieve holiness, heroes heroes because they do brave deeds. They are strictly parallel to the poets, and in all three the exemplary function is something added to and not inherent in their specific natures.

I welcome Mr Lewis's comments on Marvell's *Mower to the Glow-worms*, and his distinction between two kinds of poetry; that which seems to appeal to what is already there in ourselves, and that which introduces something alien (pp. 124–27)—and partly because in the course of them he reveals that we do in fact, as I had suspected, still mean different things by personality. 'Personality', he writes, 'must surely be a *principium individuationis*, that which distinguishes one man from another.' And it is only this second exceptional kind of poetry that deals with personality. Mr Lewis has every right to define personality in this way if he wishes, and I admit with regret that several statements in my first essay might seem to imply a similar definition. But the personality I think literature deals with is more complicated. When Mr Lewis speaks of personality being 'that which distinguishes one man from another', he seems to mean something that one personality has and no other has. But surely that is a false simplification. What distinguishes one man from another is often the degree of excellence in which he has a common human quality, or the way in which several common human qualities are blended. Even the very exceptional man will be so because he gives a new turn to the old rather than because he produces a genuine novelty. His main function is to infuse new life into the already familiar, to make wonderful once more those common human feelings which human apathy and the 'lethargy of custom' are apt to blur and to deaden. Thus Marvell's conceit of the nightingale reading the score of an air by the light of the glow-worms is his own property, no one else's, but at the same time it is inseparable from the feeling, common to any sentient human being, that life is paradoxical, full of strange absurdities, and that this very absurdity is what makes life worth living. In other words, the general truth and the personality are simply not to be separated.

In sum, though I like Mr Lewis's double division of poetry, and though I may refer to his second division later on, I do not believe personality (in my sense) to be lacking from the first kind.

I now come to Mr Lewis's attack on the Romantics for concentrating on the poet rather than on the activity of poetry. As a matter of practical policy, I agree with him heartily. The exaltation of poets into demigods is all part of the modern tendency to live vicariously; to watch semi-divine sportsmen giving exhibitions instead of playing yourself; to listen to professionals making music on the air instead of yourself acquiring a personal skill; to buy ready-cooked food in tins instead of using the domestic oven. And the wider the distance interposed between the great poet and his readers, the more inclined are the readers to be passive merely and to despair of any creative power in themselves. Poetolatry in the end can only damage the cause of poetry.

On the other hand Mr Lewis is not quite fair to the Romantics when he implies that they put the poets into a class apart. Some of them may have done; but at least Landor thought fit to include among his great men of antiquity statesmen and philosophers as well as poets, and Shelley expressly coupled the great poets and the great legislators. It would be fairer to assert that the Romantics were interested in great men (a legacy of the Renaissance), and that they directed a lot of attention to those great men who were also poets. And they may have carried the exaltation of the great individual too far. But it is unfair to say that their theory ('Naturalism', as Mr Lewis calls it) 'wants poets to be a separate race of great souls or *mahatmas*'. Separate from the man in the street, yes: but not separate from other important individuals. It was only with the rise of the Art for Art's sake theory that poets were segregated into their peculiar Holy of Holies. And to-day the Art for Art's sake school is pretty well dead.

To range ourselves against the champions of the Plain Man and to be in apparent opposition to the sound Johnsonian trust in the rightness of general opinion is distasteful and embarrassing. But I am bound to oppose Mr Lewis's protest that the ordinary man and the poet are not on different levels of feeling. Nor should I despair of Dr Johnson's support. There may be such a thing as a Plain Man ramp (see the advertisements that appeal to the Many) as there is the ramp of the Few, the Select, or the Right People (again see the advertisements and remember that the makers of a certain luxury for the Few were pleased to discover that of the Few there were so many). Disembarrassing ourselves as best we can from the opposed panics of being snobbish and of being uncritically vulgar, let us ask in what way a poet's feelings differ from those of the ordinary man. (And let me make it quite clear that poets form only a small proportion of the not-ordinary men.) First his feelings are much more interesting. The poet is Hamlet to the ordinary man's Horatio. Mr Lewis speaks of the poor show some poets have apparently made of their lives. But, to continue my analogy, the disasters which Hamlet occasioned or which befell him do not affect the matter of interest. He did far more damage than Horatio, but his feelings are much more interesting. And Dr Johnson (who after all was interested enough to write the life of that disastrous man Savage) could not deny it. It would, of course, be blasphemous to doubt the heroic potentialities in the breast of every man (I think of Arnold Bennett's remarks in the *Old Wives' Tale* on the fanatical heroism of the otherwise commonplace Mr Povey in trying to get a reprieve for his brother); but it is more often in fiction than in fact that these potentialities are allowed to take shape. The Hamlets are of a different order. Their share of the universal human potentialities has been realised in an unusual way. They make themselves available to us without the unwonted concatenation of events that forced Mr Povey's latent heroism to show itself.

Take in the second place the matter of courage. Here Mr Lewis thinks that I exalt the poet at the expense of the ordinary man. Certainly I do not wish to decry the ordinary man's courage. To watch a labourer walking coolly on a naked girder a hundred feet above the ground or to read an account of rescue work after a mine accident should fill us with astonishment. Yet the ordinary man's courage differs from the poet's. The first takes what comes his way and makes the best of the tricks of chance; the second does something different and, I think, harder. He anticipates, he 'envisages circumstance'. Shelley said that for a man to be greatly good the pains and pleasures of his species must become his own. Quite rightly he did not apply his remark to poets alone, but he sufficiently indicates the burden which the poetic imagination imposes on its owner and the resulting difference between the poet and the common man. Mr Lewis suggests that the experience of war should teach another lesson about courage, but I fancy it was this very thing that most taught me to respect the kind of courage the poets possess. Most combatants, gifted with a slightly more lively imagination than the ordinary, had to suppress it and live, without reflection or anticipation, in the moment; they merged themselves, for self-protection, with the common man, and they put up, as common men, a decent show. But to keep the imagination unimpaired was a rare and difficult achievement. It may be that no combatant achieved it fully, but a very few succeeded partially, and in so doing deserved an admiration different from that which we accord the generality. And their grade of courage was the poet's. It is true enough, as Mr Lewis says, that the ordinary man is put through it as drastically as any one else. But the point is, how does he bear the experience? It may be 'tragedy enough to be a man'; but of that tragedy different men make different things; and that is where the courage comes in.

I am not so strongly opposed to Mr Lewis as I may seem, because I have been speaking of the more considerable and consistent poets, those who approach his class of 'great men who are also poets'. And I admit that there are indeed men of very unsatisfactory lives who may, having written a few poems, go by the name of poet; and they are in an unfortunate position, lacking both the sober virtues of the ordinary man and the mental fortitude of the more considerable artist. Endowed with some imagination but deficient in stamina, they collapse under the strain of an intolerable burden. Even the more considerable poets may approximate to this class. Coleridge, the 'archangel, slightly damaged', may be the most eminent. But that description suggests the truth that angels, however damaged or debauched, may yet retain something of the angelic, which, though it may fail to make them better than the run of mankind, yet distinguishes them from it.

I have already agreed with Mr Lewis in condemning poetolatry; and I should like to repeat the condemnation to counteract any suggestion of it in the above reference to angels. On the other hand, if we refrain from thinking considerable poets the only considerable people, I cannot see much harm in paying respect to those qualities they possess in an eminent degree.

Mr Lewis (pp. 131 ff.) defines the provinces of science and poetry delightfully, and I need start no controversy on this section. I agree that the line between a poetical utterance in ordinary life and a poem is impossible to draw. But Mr Lewis appears to allow the word *poet* to be valid at a lower stage of mental distinction than I should. A skill of words giving eminence in the field of the cross-word is insufficient to qualify a man for the name of poet. Further, the notion that a man can be a great technician in words and at the same time a commonplace person is false. The words *great technician* are of course ambiguous. Mr Lewis might call a very good imitator of another's verbal mastery by this name. I should not, nor should I call him a poet either. Until a man is exceptionally skilful, not only in his range of vocabulary, his readiness at rhyming, his resourcefulness in putting things shortly or in amplifying but in his power over the sounds of words,

I should not call him a 'great technician'. And if Coleridge was right in holding that the power of music could not be acquired by mere industry, its presence must imply some superiority in the person who wields it. In other words, a 'great technician' will have some claim to be in Mr Lewis's class of great men who have also written poetry.

It is the same process of thought that makes me think that Mr Lewis's definition of poetry as an art or a skill is deficient. An art or a skill is a false abstraction and does not exist apart from the stuff on which it is exercised and the person who exercises it. And to admit it as the *differentia* of the poet does not give it any stronger claim to independent existence. To give it an existence apart from the exerciser and the stuff on which it is exercised postulates a divine act. With those who look on art as god-given I have no quarrel, but Mr Lewis does not go so far as that.

I come now to the theme in which I am most interested and about which I am least competent to speak. At the end of my second contribution I suggested to Mr Lewis that if he thinks poetry is not concerned with the poet's personality he should tell us the things poetry *is* concerned with. His reply is that poetry

> being a skill of utterance, can be used to utter almost anything: to draw attention to (though

not, of course, to demonstrate) a fact, to tell lies, to tell admitted fictions, to describe your own real or feigned emotions, to make jokes.

Later he warns us against identifying what the poet 'says' with the apparent propositions in his poem. 'The poet is not "saying" that his soul is an enchanted boat . . . what poetry "says" is the total, concrete experience it gives to the right reader.'

Mr Lewis does not appear to find anything difficult to reconcile in these two passages. But to me it is the most puzzling matter in the world, once you have jettisoned, as an affirmation, the statement that the poet's soul is an enchanted boat, to be certain that some of the items in the earlier passage, the facts, the lies, the fictions, the jokes, must not, as affirmations, be jettisoned likewise. Now it is notorious that when we speak of the subject-matter of poetry, 'the things said', or 'what poetry is about' we tend to be ambiguous. And one simple and often-made distinction may help the discussion. The phrase 'what poetry is about' may mean 'what poetry can include' or 'what it properly concerns'. That poetry may include all the items in Mr Lewis's list I freely admit, but the soul's resemblance to the enchanted boat would have to be included too. All these have their place, as means, if not on any other plea. But when these items are treated as 'what poetry properly concerns', as ends, they have a most awkward tendency to evaporate. It would be much less awkward if they evaporated altogether, but they sometimes behave like the Cheshire Cat and leave their grin behind them. One of the poems we have had occasion to discuss will illustrate well enough. This is the second verse of Marvell's *Mower to the Glow-Worms:*

> Ye country comets, that portend
>   No war nor prince's funeral,
> Shining unto no higher end
>   Than to presage the grass's fall,

and it contains a fact, namely, that the appearance of the glow-worms in the long grass indicates the approach of the hay-harvest. How far, we may ask, are these lines about this fact? Not at all far. To begin with, the fact can be stated in language remote from the poetical. Even if the poetry is about it, it is not so *quâ* poetry. Secondly, the fact is significant almost entirely through its relation to other things. There is an analogy between a glow-worm foretelling the fall of the grass by the scythe of the mower and a comet foretelling the fall of a king by the scythe of death; and there is a contrast between the miniature, rural setting of the first fall, and the celestial and political setting of the second. But these analogies and contrasts take us away from the unrelated fact of a time-congruity between appearance of glow-worms and the hay-harvest. There is yet another job of work this fact may perform through its relation to other things. The very correctness of the fact stands out against the patent falsity of the preceding and following verses, in which the nightingales read their song-books, and the mowers are rescued from will-o'-the-wisps, by the glow-worms' illumination. And once again the fact evaporates and is absorbed into something bigger, a contrast. In the end the only sense in which the poetry can be said to be 'about' the fact of a certain time-congruity as an end (the only evidence of the Cheshire Cat's grin) is that the poet may for a brief instant have been interested in it and have welcomed the opportunity of introducing it for its own sake. But even so much is doubtful, and in any case the ends which the fact serves are immensely more important to the poet than the fact in itself.

However, it would be unfair to stop at so trivial an instance. I will go on to something bigger. Mr Lewis likes stories and says that they are 'the most characteristic contents of literary utterances'.[2] I, too, can enjoy narrative

---

[2] No preference was expressed. The words quoted were intended as a purely historical statement that *in fact* most of the imaginative literature in the world is story-telling. It is a question of statistics, not of aesthetics.

verse and hope that it will not die as a literary form. But I am far from certain that even a narrative poem is about the story it narrates, in the sense of the story being the poem's end. We do not doubt that Vasco da Gama sailed round the Cape to India or that Camoens wrote an epic on that subject. And as a matter of policy it was expedient that Camoens should write under the impression that his first job was to tell a story. To have had qualms about the solidity of the story, to know that it was in danger of evaporating would have been fatal to the kind of concentration necessary to poetic composition. Even so, we have no use in ordinary action for the discoveries of the physicists about the constitution of matter. In trying to remove the mass of atoms that constitute one's body from an approaching motor-car, one does not, if one is wise, translate the physical world into terms of probability. But we do not thereby confute the physicists. Mr E. M. Forster's attack on the story element in the novel (in his *Aspects of the Novel*) is founded on this truth (that the story is insubstantial), but he applies the truth where it does not belong. It belongs to critical theory, but it need

---

Why this is so, and how stories please, are questions to which I have offered no answer. Dr Tillyard's answer, which occupies the following pages, falls, therefore, outside the controversy. He is expending critical effort in the very direction that I advise. C.S.L.

not apply to the practical realm of literary means. The idea that by using in fiction means that are apparently in closer proximity to ends, that by talking about feelings rather than exhibiting action, you are nearer perfection or closer to the true nature of the novel is chimerical. Unless fiction is a glorified essay, those feelings talked about need be no nearer the end, the total experience, than is the story element; feelings and story will have the same insubstantiality. Moll Flanders's adventures perform the same function as Lily Briscoe's yearnings over her picture in *To the Lighthouse*. And which method is right is a question not of truth but of expediency. Mr Somerset Maugham in *The Summing Up* has recently defined the nature of the story element in literature very neatly, through a comparison with the methods of painting. He pleads for the story element in the novel, but adds:

> Just as the painter thinks with his brush and paints the novelist thinks with his story: his view of life, though he may be unconscious of it, his personality, exist as a series of human actions.

What kind of existence the voyage of da Gama has when told by Camoens is far too abstruse a question for me to answer. But I feel fairly confident that for a rough description of Camoens's real, though unadmitted, ends in the poem the phrase, 'What it felt like to be alive in Portugal and its empire about the middle of the sixteenth century', would be far closer the truth than 'Vasco da Gama's voyage to India'. The notion, then, that poets tell stories is a fiction, even though it is most expedient they should act on it. It seems to me truer to describe stories in poetry somewhat in this way. The Erewhonian World of the Unborn was full of disembodied souls pestering to be allowed embodiment; and they pestered till they got two parents to consent to put up with them. So the artist's mind, when he wishes to create, is full of energy seeking an embodiment. If he is lucky he will find a story or a set of ideas that consents to perform the parental function. It is true that certain stories have a greater aptitude than others to perform that function; yet I fancy that chance plays a very important part in the choice of theme; and a poet will choose his theme not so much because it is better than a dozen others as because it happened to present itself when he was feeling creative.

Criticism can of course busy itself with the way certain stories are treated by different writers. Yet the extraordinary differences of treatment make us doubt the solidity of the stories themselves. *The Trojan Women* and the second book of *The Aeneid* both deal with the fall of Troy, but this gives them little more kinship than does the fact that they are both in verse. And that is one reason why criticism is constantly being driven to examine states of mind rather than apparent subject-matter.

How much in this I differ from Mr Lewis can be seen by his remarks on poetry and music. Poetry, he says,

> differs sharply . . . from an art like Music. You can, if you like, both make and hear a sonata without thinking of anything but sounds. But you cannot write or read one word of a poem by thinking only about poetry.

This contrast is partial, not fundamental. As regards means it is, on the whole, valid. Music need not go beyond sounds, though 'programme' music will use sounds to suggest objects or events, in life;[3] while poetry must go beyond poetry for its means. But as regards ends, music does not confine itself to sounds. The musician's brain is peopled

---

[3] I omitted programme music not because I do not like it myself but, (*a*) Because I have been given to understand that my liking for it simply proves that I am much more of a literary than a musical man. (*b*) Because it complicates the argument, when we are distinguishing literature from music, to introduce that species of music which approximates most nearly to literature. C.S.L.

with unborn souls just like the poet's, and they have nothing specifically to do with sounds; they owe their existence to the musician's total experience of life. Indeed, I should assert that poetry is most about just those things which music is most about. Not that Pater was right in saying that all art aspires towards the condition of music: for his remark implies that poetry should try to approximate its means to music's; and for poetry to fight against the heterogeneous character of its means is pure waste of energy.

For good or ill, then, although poetry is basically like music, it differs in that it shows us much more of the works. And as it is far easier to talk about the works than to define the basic experience for which those works exist, there has been, and there will be, far more literary than musical criticism. Criticism of the means of music is bound to be mainly technical, and thus to appeal to a small public. Criticism of the means of literature can range over all sorts of general interest, and can enjoy a considerable popularity. But the criticism, whether in poetry or in music, that deals with ends, with the experiences or states of mind for which these means exist, is smaller in bulk than that of means, and is exceedingly conjectural. Aristotle is typical in saying only a few words about the states of mind appropriate to tragedy, but much about the means of expressing them. Now the question of personality in poetry is a department of this difficult kind of criticism that deals with ends: and I had hoped to draw Mr Lewis on to commit himself more generally on this kind; partly because I was curious to know his views and partly because I thought I should fare better in this (as it seems to me) necessarily complementary part of our controversy, if I could induce my antagonist to commit himself first. Seeing things a different way round, Mr Lewis has (very naturally) not committed himself very far. So, since I was responsible for starting the topic, I suppose I must resign myself to saying something on it, however lamely.

And first let me repeat and have done with the notion that poetry concerns the author's personality. To render his mental pattern can be an author's object; he can need to do so; and that need is a sufficient end. (Such a rendering is valuable to many readers because, through it, they have access to important people; an access which, without it, they might be denied. This value may come from an act of sharing—it is stimulating to share something with a distinguished mind. Or the example of what a distinguished mind has made of itself may help the person who has access to it.) Exactly what percentage personality accounts for in those things which poetry is most truly about I do not feel called on to conjecture. All I can say is that personality accounts for only a part, and that it is usually interwoven with other elements.

Secondly, poetry is concerned with large general states of mind. There are many equally vague ways of putting this: universal ideas, great commonplaces, &c. Some of these states of mind recur so regularly through the ages that they appear timeless and are always easy of apprehension. The poet is bound to meet them and to want to give his version of them. And the reader enjoys it because it makes what he already knows live more intensely in his mind. We all know the class of feeling that impelled Achilles to sulk and Dido to hate Aeneas.

But not all these large general states of mind are so near to us as Achilles's anger of Dido's hatred. There are (making, if we wish, a third category) areas of feeling, near enough to the poet and felt by a number of people, which because of their remoteness from other ages, are in a different class and set to work a different part of the reader's mind; for instance, the feelings of Spenser about the house of Tudor, or of the early Icelanders about revenge, or of the early eighteenth century about enthusiasm'. All these feelings are within the compass of the normal human imagination, but they are not always equally present at all periods of history. But the poet who is contemporary with their vogue is apt to experience them with a great intensity, probably not bothering to distinguish them from feelings whose vogue is less fluctuating; and he is not content till he has given his version of them. Thus it is that the poet is also an historian, in that he can express (and this can be expressed only by artistic means) what his contemporaries felt about certain events and ideas, and what it felt like to be alive just then. That this function, though partly historical, has nothing specifically to do with the facts of history and cannot be called in the ordinary sense informative, can be seen by considering the case of music. For music can fulfill *both* functions of poetry last enumerated. Of course it does not specify the wrath of Achilles or the hatred of Dido, but it can include such feelings within itself. The music of Gregorian and Byzantine hymns or the Restoration music written for royal funerals and coronations has, in addition to a generally human, an historical interest. It tells us something of what it was like to be alive in epochs different from our own.

But there are states of mind expressed in poetry which appear remoter or stranger than anything mentioned hitherto. And here I have Mr Lewis's support; for he admits

> that there are also poems which seem to give me a new and nameless sensation or even a new sense, to enrich with experience which nothing in my previous life had prepared me for.

It is when he goes on to suggest, 'when this happens... we are sharing something peculiar to the poet' that I feel doubtful. Anyhow, I think we may get further with this type of poetry, without bringing in personality.

I would suggest that when poetry appears very strange it does so because it is about something either very new or very old. (And again, if we want them, we have two more, fourth and fifth, categories.) It is not easy to speak of either kind without opening oneself to ridicule; and of the poetry that is about something very new I speak with the greatest hesitation. However, let it be said (and with Professor Whitehead's *Adventures of Ideas* as a reference) that it might happen that new ways of feeling, destined to become widespread, appear first in spasmodic fashion among the artists.[4] To the general public they must at first appear strange: to many people both fascinating and repulsive; fascinating because suggesting adventure, repulsive because dangerous and unfamiliar. More often than not the new will appear alongside the known. Indeed, many great works of art, in other ways dealing with the familiar, may contain bits of genuine novelty. Shakespeare's last plays (which Mr Lewis mentions for their strangeness)

---

[4] I agree. Notice the appearance of the Evolutionary Idea in *Hyperion* and *The Niblung's Ring* before the spread of Darwinism. C.S.L.

may do so, and in our own time Joyce's *Ulysses*. Music could furnish examples in this category also.

Poetry which is about something very old brings us into the region of the psychologists, and especially of those who are influenced by Jung. The phrase, 'very old', however, is ambiguous. If in our infancy we do indeed pass through all the stages of human evolution we have the option of preferring the supposed feelings of infants to the supposed feelings of prehistoric man. But whichever option we choose, or if we choose both (as we may), we can reasonably speak of great antiquity. Not that all the feelings of a remote antiquity are unfamiliar to us. On the contrary, the experience of rebirth which Miss Bodkin describes as the pattern of tragedy is both primitive and very present to us; belonging mainly to the category of Achilles's wrath. But just as certain 'psychic' people are held to retain gifts once common to mankind as a whole, so it is possible for certain poets to express feelings once widespread, but giving the appearance of peculiarity. These feelings, once powerful, but dimmed by time, are analogous to those in my third category, to the feelings of Spenser about the house of Tudor, or of the early eighteenth century about 'enthusiasm'; but being so far remoter, they are felt and expressed and then recognized with greater rareness and difficulty. And in the recognition there is a greater chance of self-deception, not only because we are in a region where fact is scanty but because many of us to-day find the primitive a quick intoxicant. But though I recognize the heavy odds against being right in detecting any specific instance of primitive feelings reappearing in poetry of historical times, I feel confident of the probability that such a process does often take place. Simply as an example of the kind of thing that might happen and not with any confidence that I am not imagining what just is not there, I should like to repeat an observation made elsewhere. The following is a possible example of how feelings which must have been very widespread but which with the physical changes of the earth's surface cannot have remained in their early vivid state, reappear in the lines of a comparatively modern poet. When mankind was numerically scanty, and when the natural odds against him were large, he may have feared the wilderness in a way unknown to the Mesopotamian peasant or the medieval burgher, not to speak of a modern town-dweller. The pressure of this fear over long ages would modify mankind's cast of mind. But later this fear would recede far into the background; not so far, however, but certain men, sensitive in that direction, could resuscitate it. Such a resuscitation I have imagined I have seen in two passages of Milton, passages which strike me as more 'primitive' than anything in the Romantics, in whose poetry one would naturally look first for such a manifestation. These passages come from the Lady's description of her fears in *Comus* and Michael's account of what happened to the mount of Paradise after the Flood. The Lady says:

> *What might this be? A thousand fantasies*
> *Begin to throng into my memory*
> *Of calling shapes, and beckoning shadows dire,*
> *And airy tongues, that syllable men's names*
> *On Sands, and Shoars, and desert Wildernesses.*

And the mount of Paradise becomes

> *An Iland salt and bare,*
> *The haunt of Seales and Orcs, and Sea-mews clang.*

It may well be objected that even if the poets do resuscitate the primitive they do no good by so doing. Let man's early fears disappear like the back teeth which modern man has learnt to do without. It might be answered that we cannot afford to dispense utterly with any feeling the race has been through. Mixed with other feelings this primitive fear may enrich the total capacity of a human being: and the poets who recall it and similar feelings may be making an inestimable contribution to the fullness of life.

The states of mind described in the four last categories are universal to man, or racial, or communal, or characteristic of a particular age. Anyhow they concern many men. But when they appear in the work of the poet they will help and will be helped by the personal element. We trust what a great poet makes us feel about the age he lived in because he impresses us as a distinguished person; and we trust his own distinction partly because he is so sensitive to what goes on around him. The ever-varying interplay of the personal and the communal is one of the first attractions of poetry.

This ends my enumeration and brief discussion of some of the things poetry can be about. I hope that through them I have at least cleared myself from any suggestion that I confine the scope of poetry to personality.

Finally, I must record a very hearty agreement with Mr Lewis in his plea for the πεπαιδευμένος (as he calls him after Aristotle) or the Common Reader (as I might call him after Dr Johnson and Mrs Virginia Woolf) as the ultimate judge of poetry.[5] The principle here is like that of

---

[5] I do not intend to identify the πεπαιδευμένος (the perfect reader) with ὁ τυχών (the common reader). C.S.L.

refusing to allow the General Practitioner to be bullied by the Specialist, and like the magnificent statement I got from the lips of a French business man that the ultimate direction of business should be in the hands of other than business men. I need say no more, since Mr Lewis has made his point so well.

It is a pleasure to have ended on a note of agreement. Yet Mr Lewis is an admirable person to disagree with; and I incline to admire his arguments as much when they seem wrong as when they seem right. He is, indeed, the best kind of opponent, good to agree with when one can, and for an enemy as courteous as he is honest and uncompromising; the kind of opponent with whom I should gladly exchange armour after a parley, even if I cannot move my tent to the ground where his own is pitched.

NOTE

On re-reading my share of this book I am disquieted by the apparent lack of connexion between the accounts of poetry given in the First Essay (pp. 25, 32) and in the Fifth (pp. 131–36). In the First we are told that the poet puts together 'scraps of ordinary seeing' in such a way as to produce a new mode of consciousness. This new mode sees objects more 'synthetically', and with a 'vaster context' than we are usually able to attain. It is described as being 'racial';[1] and a subject who enjoyed it habitually would be superhuman. In the Fifth Essay poetry consists in a special use of language which exploits its extra-logical properties so as to convey the concrete.

The trouble about these two descriptions is not that they contradict, but that they do not seem to come near enough even for contradiction; it is difficult to bring them into any relation at all. But as I am not prepared to give up either (in its entirety), I must try to do so.

In a certain sense the earlier account may be said to deal

---

[1] p. 29.

with the poetical consciousness or vision, and the later with the poetic language. But the later deals very cursorily with the nature of that language and is more concerned with the objects which such language is fitted to present; i.e., with the concrete. And the first account warns us that language and perception cannot here be separated, the poetic consciousness being incarnate in the poetic words, syntax, &c. It would therefore be truer to say that the first account treats of the poetic process ('seeing' and 'saying') and the second of the poetic object or content (the thing 'seen' and 'said').

When modern scientists find it convenient, they stop talking of space and time and begin to talk of space-time. My two accounts can be combined if you will allow me to talk of seeing-saying or language-consciousness, or, for brevity, speechthought. You must understand that 'thought' here carries no specially *intellectual* connotation.

The unified description would then run as follows. The poetic speechthought does not exist permanently and as a whole in the poet, but is temporarily brought into existence in him and his readers by art. Its differentia is to be 'synthetic', to include objects in unusually rich, or wide, contexts, and to attain the concrete; and all these three mean the same.

So far, all is well. Inconsistencies begin when I go on, rashly enough, to speculate on its essential nature; I should

NOTE

have confined myself to its actual occurrence in our experience. As it is, the First Essay identifies it (i) with 'racial', and (ii) with angelic, consciousness. In the Fifth Essay it seems to be on a much lower plane. Here it looks as if the concrete were accessible to all men at all times, except when they were proving something, and poetry merely succeeded in uttering what all experienced.

Now the First Essay is clearly self-contradictory—at least only a very odd idea of 'races' and 'angels' will identify 'racial' and 'angelic' consciousness. To speak more plainly, I have assumed (i), what now seems to me very unlikely, that large groups of human individuals possess a common consciousness; and (ii) that if they do, this common consciousness would be so superior to that of the individuals that it might be called 'angelic'. In fact, I have exaggerated. All I have a right to say is that poetic speech-thought uses such memories, associations, and values as are widely distributed among the human family in space and time, and rejects what is merely idiosyncratic; and that no human being permanently enjoys poetic speech-thought. Perhaps I can still say that if any being did, he, or it, would be an angel. At any rate, a Corker.

So much for the internal incoherence of Essay I; now for the relation between I and V. I do not myself think there is a contradiction here: but to make the *threatened* contradiction quite plain I will aggravate it into the form 'I. Poetry brings into existence a mode of consciousness, that is, an experience, quite new to humanity, and otherwise inaccessible. II. Poetry merely communicates the existing experience of humanity.' The first description gives poetry a creative function, the second makes it a mere recorder.

We need not here discuss the claim that poetry is 'creative' in the strict (theological) sense of the word, for no one really believes that the poet *facit e nihilo*. But even when we have dismissed this, there remains a sharp contrast between that which develops a new experience and that which merely records an old one.

My own way out of the difficulty is as follows. The distinction between making and reporting was framed for the life of 'operation', and we are here trying to intrude it on a plane where its common-sensible meaning disappears. To make a table is one thing: to tell about it is another. Well and good. But suppose you are asked to go and look at the new table and tell us how you like it. This is a little harder. Do you just *find* your liking for the table standing there in the room like the table itself? Or is the liking slightly modified by the efforts preparatory to 'telling'? Is it in some degree produced by the desire to tell? For perhaps you would not have thought about the table at all, would neither have liked nor disliked it, if we had not asked you. Already, you see,

NOTE

the attempt to tell or report is partly making the thing to be told. Now go a step farther. Suppose you already like (or dislike) the table: we now ask you to give us the best account you possibly can of this like or dislike. That is, we ask you to summon up and hold steady what is naturally fugitive, to disentangle what is naturally mixed up with a mass of other experiences, to cleanse of incommunicable personal features what seems at first to have its whole being in such features, to regard disinterestedly what is attached in a hundred ways to your passions. We are, clearly, at the same moment, asking you to describe a given experience, and also to have a new experience.

We can now restate what seemed contradictory. Poetry does record ordinary experiences, in the sense that it expresses in their concreteness the sort of things that are happening to us all the time. But then we do not ordinarily attend to their concreteness: we are content to take most of them as mere signposts to the gratification of our appetites. To attend to them disinterestedly, to replace them in a less personal context, to correct our personal perspective, not (like the scientist) by making abstraction of hopes and fears but by turning on hope and fear themselves an impartial eye—that is to have a very new experience indeed. More briefly, poetry presents *concrete experience* (which we have every day) and, in so doing, gives us an *experience of the concrete*,² which is a very different matter. To find out what our experience has, all along, been really like, is to remake experience.

If this solution is not accepted—and I feel very far from certain about it myself—I do not think the next step is to scrap one or other of the apparently contradictory propositions. I think it would be better to go on working in the hope that we shall find a reconciliation. Each seems to me to contain something that can hardly be doubted. I cannot cease to believe either that poets paint 'the light that never was' or that they are full of 'images which find a mirror in every mind and sentiments to which every bosom returns an echo'.

In conclusion, it may be well to add that the 'novelty' or 'remaking' of experience here referred to does not mean that obvious novelty ('creation' in the sense of feigning, or invention) which is present in *The Ancient Mariner* and absent from *Vanity Fair*. I am assuming that the fictional element in poetry, the marvellous or feigned, is in some way or other a recording (though also a remaking) of actual experience. In what way, I do not now attempt to determine; the subject has been greatly neglected.

C.S.L.

---

² Readers may be helped by remembering how important the distinction between a *Succession of Perceptions* and a *Perception of Successions* has proved in some philosophies.

Discover C. S. Lewis

"If wit and wisdom, style and scholarship are requisites to passage through the pearly gates, Mr. Lewis will be among the angels."
—*The New Yorker*

Find a complete selection of C. S. Lewis titles at CSLewis.com

Available wherever books and e-books are sold

HarperOne
An Imprint of HarperCollins*Publishers*

Discover great authors, exclusive offers, and more at hc.com.

Introducing the C. S. Lewis Signature Classics
Eight Key Titles Presented Together for the First Time

HARDCOVER GIFT EDITION

PAPERBACK ANTHOLOGY

EIGHT-VOLUME BOX SET

Mere Christianity • *The Screwtape Letters* • *Miracles* • *The Great Divorce*
The Problem of Pain • *A Grief Observed* • *The Abolition of Man* • *The Four Loves*

Available wherever books and e-books are sold

HarperOne
An Imprint of HarperCollinsPublishers

Discover great authors, exclusive offers, and more at hc.com.

www.ingramcontent.com/pod-product-compliance
Lightning Source LLC
Chambersburg PA
CBHW011139290426
44108CB00020B/2690